About the author

Prachi Garg is an author, motivational speaker, and entrepreneur.

She started www.ghoomophiro.com, an enterprise where the team organizes corporate tours based on the customers' requirements, budget and provides them with a bouquet of options. Recently, Ghoomophiro expanded its portfolio for women solo travel across India and Southeast Asia.

She has delivered workshops on entrepreneurship at major B-schools across India, like FMS, IIMs, Miranda House, IMT, among others. Her startup has been covered by CNN and other leading media. She has also authored the 'Super' series, which comprises of three books. *Superwomen* talks about the journeys of women entrepreneurs and has been constantly topping the non-fiction charts at various bookstores. *SuperCouples* lists couple-preneurs and their journey of balancing the relationship and work. *Supersiblings* is the third in this series and captures the essence of siblings and their startup together. Her first fiction work titled *The Legends of a Startup Guy* – that charts out the initial stages of hiccups of a startup and an entrepreneur – is one of the Amazon best reads. Taking the whole narrative a step forward, her book *Startup Secrets from the Ramayana* is her latest gig around mythology and entrepreneurship.

Apart from being an MBA graduate from Great Lakes Institute of Management, Chennai, she is a distinguished alumna from Miranda House.

@prachimadri @Prachi1905 /Authorprachigarg

Praise for the author and her works

" ...[Superwomen] unleashes the secret of achieving your passion... perfect combination of emotion and intelligence."

– *Women's Era*

" ...[for] youngsters looking for inspiration, this might be the one."

– *Hindustan Times*

" Interesting journey of how 20 women played fantastic roles towards perfection..."

– *Millennium Post*

" ...must read book for all newbie entrepreneurs."

– *The Times of India*

STARTUP SECRETS FROM THE *Ramayana*

PRACHI GARG

Srishti
Publishers & Distributors

SRISHTI PUBLISHERS & DISTRIBUTORS
Registered Office: N-16, C.R. Park
New Delhi – 110 019
Corporate Office: 212A, Peacock Lane
Shahpur Jat, New Delhi – 110 049
editorial@srishtipublishers.com

First published by
Srishti Publishers & Distributors in 2020

10 9 8 7 6 5 4 3

Printed and bound in India

Dedicated to
my father Brejesh Garg,
and mother Neeru Garg.

Contents

Acknowledgement

This book has been possible due to the enormous love and support that people have given to me. It was their constant support that kept me going and ensured that I should be able to deliver it on time. I would like to thank everyone for making the journey smooth for me.

Family members play a great role in making such accomplishments possible. In my case as well, this holds true. Each one of them has been instrumental and has been there when required.

Mr. Arup Bose from Srishti Publishers for his faith in my concept and agreeing to publish the same.

Stuti, my editor, who undertook the tedious task of going through my manuscript, editing it and coming out with exciting ideas.

All my friends who provided me with constant moral support to make this happen.

All the readers of *Superwomen*, *SuperCouples*, *SuperSiblings* and *The Legends of a Startup Guy*, whose love inspired me to pen down *Startup Secrets from the Ramayana*.

1

Introduction

As he stood wondering in a foreign land, looking around the sight of complete mayhem, Ram stood at peace with himself. He had been through the worst; it was only a matter of time now before things settled down. His now agitated site would settle down with the new ways of the affair. For years, Ram had worked really hard and strategically to take over this company. He had been watching and waiting, patiently, waiting for the right time, with the right allies, to strategically make his move in the boardroom, striking when the iron was hot, to take over this resource management firm across the sea. Lank.co had been a strong and steady enterprise that had been growing aggressively under the strong leadership of Ravan. He was a well-established businessman, who was trying to push into the Indian market, where Ram was already working hard to gain market monopoly and earn everyone's confidence. After all the failure he had left behind, Ram was not willing to lose his hold on the game yet again. This time, he was determined to keep a steady head on his shoulders and work in a way that would take together everyone, building the team and watching out for competitors and trouble-makers.

It had been a long and hard fourteen years since he had left behind that known territory, the comfort of home, and most importantly, the embarrassment of failure. Honestly, it had not even been his own failure, but that of his associates.

"Never again am I trusting people to take critical decisions without getting approval from me first!" He had sworn as he took back the last boxes from his office in Ayodhya. His heart had ached in handing back the keys to the building owners, not just because he felt let down, but because there were so many others counting on his business and skills, trusting in him for their small-scale startups and family businesses. Ram had been the next door go-to guy for everyone who wanted anything to do with business administration. After all, the kid had graduated with a gold medal from the most premium management institute of the country. If there was any problem related to businesses in Ayodhya, Ram had an answer for it.

"Why don't you make a business out of this, brother ?" His younger sibling Lakshman had brought this up one day, watching Ram sit and give advice to the owner of the oldest architecture firm of the city. "It seems like a legit opportunity. You give people industrial advice, help them kick-start their businesses, maybe even raise funding for them if necessary, and charge a percentage for your efforts." Lakshman was an avid fan of his elder brother, his closest friend and the most loyal companion. After much deliberation, the brothers had set up their little business consultancy firm in Ayodhya. They would help with market research, analytics, setting up business and financial models, and even providing funding support, if needed, to the uprising businesses in and around the city.

It had been a smooth ride. This was a unique business, and more importantly, it was one that addressed the massive gap of lack of understanding or knowledge of the business world in the simpletons of Ayodhya. Before long, Lakshman and Ram were running around, neck deep in work, juggling multiple projects and trying to comprehend friends from enemies amidst the chaos of home-town people, who all leaped to him for help and favours.

There were moments of a strange kind of pressure too, mostly from the people he dearly loved and respected. "Oh, Ram! Look, my son is going through a rough phase in his little store. But I am sure you won't refuse him a little money till he recovers, would you? He will pay you back later!" His aunt Kaikeyi would come running to him with a sorry face. And she was not alone. Anyone who knew Ram, did not need to unravel any mystery to figure out what a simple, kind-hearted man he was, who could not refuse a request or turn a needy down.

"You must not cultivate this kind of an impression, big brother!" Lakshman would always warn him. "In the business world, where there is such cut-throat competition, you will have to take some tough decisions, otherwise everyone will take you for a ride! Brother, you have to use discretion; be smart about who you allow into the inner circle and reveal your actual ideas to. Trust me, the world is not as utopic as you think it to be." Lakshman had the same education and upbringing as Ram, and yet he was the more practical out of the two. Ram, on the other hand, was an idealist, who believed in the larger goodness and felt duty-bound to give whatever he had for the betterment of anyone who sought it.

"Come on, Lakshman! You do not have to be so pessimistic about the world! I believe in hope… the more you inculcate it, the more it brings joy into the world." Ram would speak, beaming with optimism. Great quality in a person, but not very lucrative for a businessman, quite frankly!

As Ram's name and business prospered, his fame reached all nearby cities and towns in the state. It even began spreading to a larger part of northern and southern India. With his growing work, his responsibilities and consequential liabilities also grew; what with how little Ram cared about how much profit or margins he was keeping for himself.

For a young Indian man to be respectable, doing well for himself professionally and yet managing to stay single is humanly impossible. Even before he had begun getting comfortable with the consultancy firm, Ram was being bombarded by close friends and relatives about how it was only appropriate for him to take the next obvious step in life – to choose a suitable soulmate. By suitable, they meant one that mostly fit the physical and material standards of his stature, of course. Like most soft-hearted Indian youth, Ram could not ward off the preying eyes of the older relatives, and finally had to give in. "Fine, I will get married. But I will find a suitable bride for myself, and no one will pressurize me into rushing to a decision," Ram gave his final word, which, to his immense surprise, was followed without a single question.

As time passed, he signed up for some online dating and matrimonial apps. "Looking for someone whose intellect can impress me, as much as my soul should impress hers," his profile said. For the looks and the name he carried, Ram often received right swipes. And yet, he found not a single person who held his attention on a chat longer than five minutes.

"You have to be more open !" Kaushalya would try to convince him to explore his idea of what he thought was a perfect soulmate. "You can't just sit here and wait for the perfect woman to walk right into your life." Ram would nod and smile, not wanting to contradict his mother's advice. Despite not being a romantic, Ram deeply believed that whatever was destined for him would happen naturally, and that there was nothing he could think of better than to let his fate drive his mind.

Handling multiple things at the work and professional front, along with looking after his family, often had Ram on the go. Along with Lakshman, he would make several short trips in between weekends to meet his clients and address their issues in person, if they were not satisfied with conference or video calling counselling. It was on one such trip that the brothers had to extend their stay beyond the intended week, and decided to do something recreational over the weekend, till the next scheduled meetings resumed. Ram searched up a bit, and finally decided to go to a local arts café, where an exhibition was in progress. It was here that he saw Sita, surrounded by many young men and women, as she delivered her talk on ethics in business. It was a small informal group where young intellects had gathered together to discuss about the upcoming expo.

"Oh my god ! It is like I am hearing a female version of you talk about all these principles and ethical choices you keep blabbering about, brother!" Lakshman had said in awe, as he pulled up a chair to join the group. Ram quickly and silently followed. As the discussion steered towards choices between what is right and what is good, Ram felt compelled to contribute and contradict Sita's former argument. "If I may, the two need not be mutually exclusive. In fact, one may often find that with due diligence and a slight inconvenience, it is possible to adopt and execute both – the right and the good – for the business. Take the example of all the new pool cab apps. Not only are they creating a lot of market for shared taxi, but are also trying to resolve the pollution and traffic crisis." Ram spoke highlighting what he felt was a great example of modern day ethically sound business products. It was like an instant connection. A perfect magnetism that attracted two people. Sita heard Ram speaking in his usual strong and poised composure and was immediately drawn to his conversation. It was perhaps then that they both knew they would end up respecting each other way more than just being attracted.

Before long, the mutual admiration took the form of love and brought the couple into a conjugal relationship. Things could only have grown better from there; or at least that's what they often thought. Unfortunately, that is not what happened.

Standing on the fiftieth floor of the newest takeover of Lank.co, Ram thought about all that had gone south, despite all assumptions and predictions. Ayodhya, that had become Ram's proclaimed kingdom in business management, was in the grip of his palms – his loyal customers, family, and associates. It had felt like all dreams were now a reality. Until they were not. When ambitions started overstretching, boundaries began melting and favours turned out to be over-promising. Ram could not have imagined up until the big wave hit him, that he would be so instantly betrayed and uprooted by those who he thought to be his closest!

2

The Value of Disruption

The so-called faults in one's destiny can generally be traced back to a culmination of errors, short-sightedness and ignored signs. It does not matter then, when people tell you that you had a serious bad luck or that it was god's will. Because, in all probability, it was god's will for you to open your eyes, see what was going on and make informed, educated decisions based on all the facts and resources provided to you. Perhaps that part could be credited to destiny.

It was no different for Ram and his incredible work journey in Ayodhya. There was no doubt that he had employed his good business sense and market understanding into a space that had an obvious demand for his skills. What Ram seriously overlooked was the source he most put his faith in – people.

"I thought you relished in being a people's person, Ram," Sita had questioned him as they had sat down one day, reviewing their last quarter reports. "It turns out that these very people are better at dealing with you than you are with them." As bitter as Sita's words may have sounded, they were true. After all, she did not have anything she needed from Ram. She was probably one of the few people who spoke the truth when it came to letting Ram know of his follies and past mistakes. The rest of the people were either there for some vested interest or simply for the show, neither of which scenarios provided for any incentive in speaking the truth.

Truth can be your biggest strength and the lack of it, a brutal enemy. Ram, blinded by his faith in people, went about his principles of philanthropic business. While excelling in his consultancy was his priority, doing that in a manner as to benefit his clients often took precedence. Which was great, except it often took precedence over his own interest, often his own budgets and at several occasions, at the risk of loss on a personal level.

"Honestly, it is not even that which bothers me, Ram. Because I know that the business makes enough to sustain these minor injuries caused by your philanthropy," Sita had told him during a confrontation she and Lakshman had planned, to help Ram see the other side of the story.

"Well, as long as the injuries can be contained, I don't see any harm done," Ram had refuted.

"With all due respect, Ram, do you know what they call you in the market? I am not talking about those devout old school runners of the city who have known you as a child. They call you Mr Perfect, everyone knows that. But do you know what the new-age businessmen, with their heads and hearts craving for any means to dupe the world call you?" Ram stared at Lakshman in response to the rhetorical question. It couldn't possibly be a good name, if it made Lakshman so angry. But it had been too long since he had been ignorant. It had cost him enough. It was now time that Ram faced the music, the same that he had muted for all these years.

"They call me Mr Gullible." Ram had heard the rumours and only chosen to ignore them for the sake of his faith in humanity, which unfortunately, had been diminishing consistently over the years in business.

The origin of misuse of Ram's goodwill had seemed pretty harmless. A favour here, an exemption there, all for those who were not doing so well in business. "Oh Ram, only you can get me out of this quicksand. I don't have any money to pay you, but my generations will thank you for saving our lives." It would have been difficult to think that one could fall for such theatrics, but it was Ram. He had a way of finding some light in his heart, even for the worst of people. Concessional rates, free favours, prioritising 'urgent' assignments that turned out strategic to beat the competition, manipulated references and regularly bouncing checks. The list was endless. At one level, these increasing queues of favours were clogging productive output as well as inflow of deserved cash, which could still be blocked or compensated for with better performance in business. But at another, more crucial level, the internal organisational structure was getting affected by 'favoured' hiring.

"Please, Ram. My son will never get a job. We have bills to pay. Why don't you teach him?" This went on. Despite his sincere efforts for building a professional culture, Ram's firm was getting soaked with people who had no ambitions, skills or the resemblance of the core values of the organisation. Ram's empire was growing in several ways, but not necessarily in a sustainable and holistic manner, with a foundation strong enough to hold the heights and would soon bring the whole set-up crumbling down.

"I cannot believe this is happening!" Lakshman was flabbergasted. "How does your landlord have a hold of the organisation? I can understand the property is in his name. But we can simply move between another set of walls, right?" The quiet room where Ram, Sita and Lakshman stood shook in confused silence. "Except that the whole organisation has been mortgaged in the name of paying off loans. I should have known. Our aunt Kaikeyi was not only looking to get her son to join the family business, but also have him take over the financial control in lieu of having us use the property for free for the first year." The plot had been a simple and evil one. Three years ago, Kaikeyi had donated the property to Dashrath, Ram's father, for Ram and Lakshman to build their office in, for free, if they would take her son Bharat in as an apprentice. What had started as harmless tutoring had turned into Kaikayi's malignant plan of digging out all the details of the organisation, always conversing with Dashrath on the pretext of showing concern, having Bharat take over the finances, and then, with charges of property debts, having Ram to sign over a mortgage. What the unsuspecting entrepreneur had not anticipated was the hidden clauses in the contract that gave her the power to transfer the proprietorship of the firm in Bharat's name at the slightest delay in payments.

"Of course, there were going to be payment delays. Have you seen the insane amount of delays most of our clients cause in paying their fees? After all, it is Ram they are dealing with. He would never hurt a fly!" Lakshman sounded more helpless than angry. He knew his brother's heart was in the right place, but it was the place that had caused them to stand ousted from their own office, outridden from their own firm.

"Let's go!" Ram said in a dignified yet tired tone. "There is nothing left here, but mistakes. We have to pick up what we can and walk on." He spoke, locking the last of the locks, taking out the key that hung around his neck for safe keeping.

"I am never going to forgive Bharat for this," Laksham was beside himself with frustration.

"But this is not even his fault," Sita tried to rationalise with him. There was a reason Ram and Sita had formed this emotional and intellectual connection. They thought and felt the same way, with rational arguments and principles over impulses. "There is no doubt that Kaikeyi's plan employed Bharat. But he was just a pawn. He did not really know he was being used to this end result." She was right too. There was more blame and ownership to be taken by Ram, Sita and Lakshman than anyone else, because they had let themselves be ignorant and gullible. That is not how businesses are run. Being ethical is often confused with being a simpleton. But the two do not have to be mutually inclusive.

"In hindsight, nothing should have come as a surprise," Ram spoke to Lakshman and Sita, his strongest and most loyal confidants, as they sat on their regular rendezvous spot, away from the bustling city crowd. While on the one hand, the trio had accepted graciously what they admitted as their mistake, on the other hand, an urgent and in-depth debriefing was imperative. "Let us break things down to understand what all went down."

Brainstorming had always been a big help. Ram believed that exchange of ideas, from all levels of experience and competence was the way forward. That is what they had done from the beginning. An establishment of democracy within the organisation as well as outside, in both back end and front end. "One of the first mistakes we made was not setting up a definitive and balanced policy in dealing with each other and others." Ram began with putting things down in black and white, figuratively speaking. "The moment there is a policy brought to place, it gives a direction and a guideline to things that you will otherwise not give a thought to. It would also give you the space to impose a standard and get away with being stubborn about it, especially for people like me, who have a hard time saying no to people."

"I am sorry; my hands are tied by the policies," Lakshman spelt it out. "That is what we should have done for all the people who came asking for exemptions or favours."

Although not being able to say no to people was not the only problem that caused a downfall for Ram and Co., it still had proved to be a major cause. "Another thing we should have been extremely cautious about is the kind of commitments we made to people. We were rather indiscriminate with our planning and priorities. There should be an organised pipeline, based on workload, value of return and the long term goals with the third party," Sita added her two-pence. She had been at the receiving end of the music for this one. Ram and Co. had had the reputation of entertaining just about anybody as a client, with no monitory or business quality filters. To put it crudely, they had no standards when it came to picking up assignments or planning their approach. Instead, they just went about taking assignments from whoever came knocking at their door, asking for whatever help needed, without really negotiating for costs. "I don't think we even had quarterly planning. We were just doing good business, getting better at what we do and continuously increasing our outreach." Sita only highlighted what should have been evident to the entrepreneurs from the beginning, as Ram had already mentioned. This had been their shortsightedness, especially in the light of setting up a quality of client and portfolio to boast of.

What made matters even more disturbing was that while Ram and Co. had been earning constant money from prominent and recurring clients, their financial planning had been down the hill. Again, his reputation had played a very important role for both ends of the spectrum. "We have had recurring clients, we have built loyalty and we have had some of the most reputable names in the city approach us for business consultancy, without negotiating on the price. This just goes on to say that we were on the right track as far as quality of service and client engagement is concerned," Lakshman pointed out.

"But there was a persistent financial problem, wasn't there?" Sita, the consistent voice of reasoning amidst the trio, popped for further probing. The response was predictable. Ram and Co. had spent a lot more on sustaining themselves and the resources they had spent on their clients than the cumulative profit they had made from paying customers. Ram's philosophy of delivering the best led to a genuine expense hike, and his generosity often led him to charging a lot less than he should have.

Thus, this culmination of financial debts, reputation of being gullible and the shortsightedness of bad judgments had brought the trio to a point of shutdown, from their own hometown, in their own business, by those they had trusted the most. What were the options in front of them now? They could fight back, beating their heads and hands against iron walls of technically flawed arguments. After all, the contracts had been signed in ink by the unsuspecting Ram himself. There was always the moral high ground where they could try to bring Bharat to. But that argument was flawed in its foundation because of the lack of a moral high ground in the first place. The only plausible solution that would help them with any restoration of confidence and the remaining of their respect would be to graciously admit defeat and move on.

"I have made up my mind. If this is the course that is driving us, I vote that we ride along, find ourselves in a place and time that gives us the liberty to learn from our mistakes and start afresh." Ram was finally sounding like the strong and confident man his people knew him to be – unshaken, unbent by the follies and defeats.

"I am with you in this, Ram, till the very end. I suggest we start from ground zero. But it will have to be in a place where we are not known, lest people try to play the same games with us all over again," Sita was just as determined.

There was no doubt that Lakshman would be joining them in this journey to unknown roads too. "We have done this once. I am sure we can do it again. This time, with more caution and better preparation." It was settled then. The trio would leave Ayodhya and explore the space further away from their reputation.

It is the theory of disruption that Ram had learned from his guru, Shiva – his mentor and a major business merger speciality, who had led to several organisations diluting to be reborn as new identities. Shiva had often told Ram about this theory that asked seekers to be willing and daring enough to disrupt what they believe in or had built, to create chaos and destruction of their assumptions and prejudices formed out of experiences and knowledge, only to start all over again. "This is the way of steering clear from complacence and carelessness," he would say. "In the journey of life, it is often the easier choice to stay where you are, continue with what you know and feel happy with the way things are running in your life. But remember, the day you stop running your life and let it run you, is the day you begin to decay." Valuable words for an entrepreneur, just as they are for anyone seeking something meaningful from life. It was not the easy choice then, but the choice that Ram, Sita and Lakshman made – leaving their beloved city of Ayodhya, their established firm, their families and the complacency of the known. They headed out to a neutral ground for discoveries.

"I already see this as an opportunity to diversify." Ram was talking as the trio sat at the airport, diligently looking up avenues and collaborations online, a homework they thought might come in handy when they landed at their destination. "Instead of having clients from and around Ayodhya come to us, we will take ourselves and our services to the client. We will get more scalable and accessible that way." That made a lot more sense. There were so many queries Ram and Co. had encountered in the past several years, which they had to deny because of geographical limitations. "This actually gives us a chance to customize our services into a more modernistic model, where we can deliver overseas at affordable costs, because we meet the clients halfway!"

"Ram, I am so glad I found you here. I thought I would never see you again!" Everyone turned their heads to see a dishevelled Bharat standing right behind them, teary-eyed and obviously distraught.

"Bharat, what are you doing here? What do you want from us?" Lakshman could not stop himself from lashing out. Sita held his arms and reminded him of himself.

Ram needed no such reminders. The sight of his once beloved and now troubled friend and almost brother made his heart melt. He rushed to Bharat's side and took him into an embrace. "No words are necessary, brother. I know you did not intend this. I hold no grudges against you. I only wish you well in the future."

Bharat broke down at the sound of such love and kindness. Ram's reputation, just as his generosity, remained untainted. "What future do I have without your hands on my shoulders? What is Ayodhya for me? How will I ever look myself in the eyes, let alone others, after what has happened?"

Sita could not hold her tears back anymore either. Bharat had been a comrade in arm; they had struggled for many clients together and had been together through thick and thin. "As long as you are not ashamed of yourself, no one else can point a finger at you," Sita endorsed Ram's words

Bharat tried his best to convince the trio to come back, suggesting ways to release the firm and to reinstate the old team. But he also understood that he was talking to empty spaces. "So be it, Ram. But I promise you this. I will run this company as you did. It will still be known as Ram and Co. and it will always wait for its Ram. I will only hold the ground and uphold your reputation till you find it fit to forgive me and return to this very place…"

Ram, Sita and Lakshman got up with their bags and as the boarding gates opened, Ram turned back to Bharat for a small pat on his shoulders, leaving him with the seal of his logo, and an assuring nod to have him know that there was trust between them. The trio left for an unknown land, to pursue an unknown journey where they had many ups and downs awaiting them.

It is not very difficult to build a venture. What takes foresight and understanding is sustaining your enterprise, understanding its strengths and weaknesses and not being afraid to admit when the efforts are not giving returns. There is immense value in disruption; it takes you away from complacence and allows to make space for bigger and better developments ahead. The reason why it is extremely critical to learn from your mistakes is so that you do not repeat them again. To admit your fault helps you move out of your comfort zone, re-establish yourself with a new identity, removed from the hangover of the past.

3

Networking is Getting the Work Done Even Before it has Begun

"Oh, I couldn't possibly take money from you, sir!" Kewat backed away from Ram and moved towards his taxi. "You have already done so much for my family, given employment to my son. It will be a sin to charge you for a ride."

Ram smiled gently and put a hand on Kewat's shoulder. "Brother, first of all, call me Ram. And secondly, I am not doing you any favour. I needed a service, and your son was a suitable candidate to look after our office. This is not a sin, this is the thumb rule of business!" Kewat stared at him helplessly. Ram had been a blessing to his family that had been on the verge of bankruptcy.

When the trio moved to the new city, they had begun by looking for a suitable space to settle into and set up their new business idea. Kewat had picked them up from the airport and driven them around for the next few days.

"Kewat, you have been such a gentleman to us these past few days; we would have been quite in a soup without you!" Sita, being her friendly, genuine self, expressed on a ride to the shortlisted office site.

Their driver had humbly smiled back into the rearview mirror. “This is the least I can do to help you out. If there's anything I can assist you with, I would be happy to contribute.”

Ever since the old man had found out that Ram's father belonged to his neighbouring village, Kewat had developed an affinity with him, Sita and Lakshman, offered to ferry them around the city of Chitrakoot and its neighbouring towns, while they searched for the right places to stay and work, the right people to talk to, to establish a foundation and to understand their market.

“Oh, Ram could befriend and make a fan even out of a squirrel, I tell you!” Sita had joked with Lakshman one evening as the trio sat down for dinner, discussing the candidature of Kewat's son as their office administrator. “I think he is reliable, holds the right skill-set, is multifaceted and has no rigidity about work timings.” Ram had established in short.

“What is even better is that we have done a thorough background check and it feels like there's little that may spring as a surprise for us,” Lakshman added his share of inference. That was probably where Ram's networking skills showed best of their colours. He matched the level of the person he was talking to, exhibited genuine interest in listening to them instead of simply talking about himself, and went the extra mile to show support to the person he felt was worth investing in.

“They're not fans, Sita…” Ram had responded to her joke eventually. “People are always looking for support and companionship and find themselves alone in the fact that they cannot find trust or comfort, despite being surrounded by people. Amidst all the isolation and distrust, it is just a nice feeling to connect with people and to find assurance that someone's got you." Both Lakshman and Sita gave a knowing, silent smile. It is, after all, the crux of all successful businesses. Nay, of all successful relationships in the world. You have to reach out to the other, let them trust you and thereafter, encourage them to let you in. Without that, any transaction is a very limited, short-lived and superficial equation. As an entrepreneur in the business world, just as an extension of the whole world, you need to understand the significance of building equations with people. "That, my dear friend, is networking," Ram said in a way that was a defining moment for the new enterprise that Ram, Sita and Lakshman were set to build thereon.

During their exploration in the wide and diverse city of Chitrakoot, the trio had come across several businessmen, several skill sets and even a whole set of freelance workers who were doing something independently or working in small sets to sustain themselves.

"The whole range of service opportunities here is mesmerising." Lakshman had exclaimed. "So many small scale entrepreneurs are bubbling all around us!" It was true. There were HR consultants, designers, engineers, fitness consultants… the whole range!

"And yet, they all feel so broken and unaccomplished, as if there is not enough opportunity. Even though there are plenty of business opportunities in each of these sectors," Sita inferred from having assessed the market in the last month or so.

Ram had been listening to this back and forth for a while. It had been clear to him from the very beginning. This was, in fact, one of his strongest learnings from his business days in Ayodhya. "The problem is with sustenance. Small businesses cannot afford to float on their own, and to increase their business, they need to make investments they cannot afford. The vicious cycle goes on." He had seen enough chefs, interior designers, coders and writers sink because they did not have a proper set up to attract clients. Some did not even have the proper infrastructure to support their projects. "What skill needs is exposure and that exposure comes with the right kind of platform… that's where we step in." Ram came into full presentation mode and Sita and Lakshman knew instantly that it was time to get brainstorming and take notes!

Building on his idea of people needing support and collectivism, Ram had come up with the idea of setting up his own co-working space. "We will call it 'Kutumb', which will be like a home to the world. There are so many people here who could use the infrastructure. We can offer them at an affordable price. What's more, we are also giving them an opportunity to collaborate and network with a whole new level of business world that they could not have done individually." Ram's idea of a co-working space had obviously been built on his fundamental ideology of connecting with people.

"Now that's what I call an ethically exciting business idea!" Sita could barely contain herself.

The idea of a co-working space was not only a clutter breaking entrepreneurial move, it was also the need of the market. "If you've been in business long enough, you know there is no such thing as ground zero. Every person you meet, every place you go to and every lesson you learn, brings you closer to a stronger and more diverse network. Which is why I cannot emphasise enough on meeting and greeting people." Ram spoke as the trio headed to buy equipment for their co-working space.

At the store, they were greeted by the old and yet enthusiastic service lady, Shabri, who was assigned to them. "Wow, Shabri, you seem to have a lot of knowledge about these equipment. It must have taken years of experience to get you to this insight." Ram always acknowledged expertise where it was due. Not just because it got him what he wanted, but simply because he felt that it was the right thing to do!

Shabri, as any human would, felt comforted and encouraged by this acknowledgement. "Let me show you what I deem my personal favourites amidst the collection. The seating arrangements are this way…" She took them to each and every section, personally testing all hardware before adding the models to the list. "I can't possibly have you take a defective product; that wouldn't be acceptable to me!" Shabri's dedication and commitment to selling only the right product was enlightening.

"We need somebody like that to collaborate with. Even a customer care representative can leave a long lasting impression, if they do it the right way." Ram thought out loud. Indeed, Shabri was somebody they signed up with right away for all future deals for hardware and equipment for Kutumb – which was going to be their startup. A co-working space where they would promote several small scale entrepreneurs and freelancers to come and work together on independent projects and collaborate on larger endeavours together.

On the one hand, as Kutumb began taking shape into a well-designed, well-structured co-working space, Lakshman, Ram and Sita, on the other hand, began focussing on recruitment and contact building, respectively. "As outsiders, it will not be easy for us to plant ourselves here without the support of those who belong here. Only then will people feel at home in our business," Ram had advised both Lakshman and Sita while setting off to talking to people in the city. "That is why I never refuse when people come asking us to participate in local festivals, or when they want some money as contribution for such rituals. This is how you build acceptability." It was one of those days when Ram was hanging out at a local tea shop, talking to the workers who were constructing the new panels in the office space. "What is the best project you have worked on in this city?" He asked them.

"Have you heard of the oldest business family in the neighbouring state, Kishkinda? Sugriva and Bali used to run the real estate business there. We constructed their whole residential compound. The families, the employees, everyone used to live there at one point." One of the construction workers went on to talk praises of the once mighty family. "But greed can be the worst of all enemies, Ram," he continued. "The brothers fought over some share distributions, and the next thing we know, Sugriva was made to pack his bags and come here, with very little money in his account, ousted from all his share in the business!"

This got Ram to ponder. He had often come across Sugriva in other business gatherings. He was working on small, insignificant projects, albeit persistently and never once meddled with another's affair. It was then that Ram made a decision to befriend the most powerful of business stalwarts of his new home ground.

"But we thought you'd approach Bali for support, Ram!"

Lakshman was exclaiming with frustration. "He is the one with capital. He has all the right contacts and he can get us a lot of business!" Contrary to what Lakshman had believed, Ram had gone ahead and brought Sugriva on-board as their operations head.

"You have to look at the bigger picture here, brother. Sugriva is the one in need and he is the one who has been wronged. He is motivated, honest, sincere, and has much higher stakes. What good would it do bringing on-board a man who could betray his own brother for business?" That made sense.

With Sugriva on Ram's side, it was becoming possible to interact with those on his side and those who thought Bali to be ethically in the wrong. More importantly, as Ram had projected, a man of as high virtues as Sugriva gave his best shots and began working on all of his connections to bring them on to the co-working space. "I know a whole troupe of other people who lost their jobs because of Bali's arrogance. I have worked with them and know that their loyalty and passion lies with me. If you think it's a good idea, I can get Sita to get on a training program with them and have them acquired for sales and customer care." Sugriva's first inputs after joining had been strong enough to bring on-board a whole bunch of interns. "Not only is this going to help with the endless tasks at hand, but also going to bring Ram a team that can be reliable and not cost a whole lot of money," he had offered to the management.

With the team coming together, the trio had begun acquiring clients in the form of freelancers, small scale entrepreneurs and people interested in collaboration. Each day, there were several enquiries and visits from people who sought an interest, either in renting out in Kutumb itself or in some or the other form of investment. "We should get the interns to first filter the applications and then bring us the shortlisted list of applications," Sita had suggested one night, as the trio sat through the night, filtering business requests.

Over a year into business now, Kutumb had been doing pretty well for itself. There had been a few collaborations which had let Ram to provide holistic services by the freelancers who had come together at the co-working space. Word had been spreading far and wide and venture capitalists often came in to look for franchise. Therefore, spreading of load share amidst the interns would really help with the burden.

"Are they capable of taking such critical decisions?" Lakshman had been a little apprehensive. After the whole Ayodhya fiasco, he had learned to take each step with caution. He was not about to mess up this time, just because his brother was too trusting.

"I trust the group. Besides, how else will you help in capacity building if you don't start trusting the young minds with simple things? A small task today will lead to a big project tomorrow!" Sugriva had full confidence in his team and took their participation very seriously.

This was something Ram had picked up on and allowed to develop. As an entrepreneur, he followed the same mantra that he did as a person – to be open to learning, even from people who were young, inexperienced, or conventionally thought to be lacking a vision. "You never know what you might be missing from your height that someone close to the ground will be able to see closely," he always advised Lakshman.

It was decided then. The team would do the first round of screening of applications and pass them on to the leadership. To

Lakshman's surprise, this started showing immediate results. Not only was the young group of interns fast and efficient in background checks, methodical circulation and passing up of relevant applications, it also gave him, Ram and Sita ample time to focus on the bigger things in Kutumb. Soon, the team of interns had built enough capacity and their own pool of resources to take initiatives. Hanuman, one of Ram's closest interns, even came up with a whole automated category app that could compartmentalize the applications based on the nature of their business and thereby move them up or down on the priority ladder. "Ram, there is this one application that has popped up on my radar. This lady named Shrupanakha is very keen on making an investment in Kutumb…" Hanuman came in to share as the top leadership were holding a meeting about branching out.

"Well, this couldn't be better timed, as we speak of decentralizing," Lakshman spoke in enthusiasm.

"What is the hold up then, Hanuman?" Ram could tell something was bothering the junior research lead. He encouraged Hanuman to speak freely.

"I don't know if I am being silly here, but something doesn't feel right. I cannot verify her background and I am not sure if her application is genuine."

Ram smiled with understanding. "There's no silliness in being thorough, Hanuman. I am glad you brought this to our attention. Please forward her application here and we will see if she is worth the interest." Hanuman left, feeling both encouraged and relieved at being taken seriously.

A few days later, Shrupanakha, who the brothers had turned down in the very first phone call, came striding into the Kutumb office. "What is she doing here? I thought we rejected her on the basis of lack of credibility!" Lakshman frowned with a questioning look.

Ram waited patiently as Shrupanakha floated around the office, asking to be connected to the head of the organisation. "Let us hear her out, Lakshman. Whatever we do, we must not lose our patience…"

Three hours and several rounds of discussion later, the brothers were still certain they did not want any form of partnership with Shrupanakha. There was a clash of ideology; she was aggressively arrogant, and above all, most of what she was saying did not fall into place with logic.

"I am telling you, you are both making a huge mistake here. I have contacts in really high places. If you do not do business with me, I will not let you flourish here in Chitrakoot!"

That just about bust the remaining shred of Lakshman's patience. He sprang out his chair, picked up Shrupanakha's application and tore it to bits. Bellowing in a voice louder than anyone had ever heard, he spoke each word with emphasis, "You will leave the premise now… and if you try to threaten my brother again, it will not end well for you!"

Throwing a fit of her own, Shrupanakha scuttered out of the office, muttering to herself some words that could not have meant well.

The silence that followed in Kutumb was enough to send across the message loud and clear. Nobody was allowed to mess with Ram, especially in front of Lakshman. Shrupanakha could not win the duo's trust, despite trying so hard. This was out of character even for Ram, but they had made up their mind. Perhaps, it was the beginning of a business battle or something more with the first ever enemy that the brothers had made.

Upon his return to the office, when Hanuman asked Ram why he had done what he did, Ram explained, "Trust is a precious investment you make in people. When I trusted you, I made one based out my intuition, experience and your deliverance. While associating yourself with the right people can bring you great joy, associating with the wrong kind can bring you a lot more harm than any battle you may have to fight against them." That was the thing about Ram; he could be so approachable and friendly with one set of people and so stoic and unwilling with another. This was what made people his best friends or his worst enemy… which was which, they were soon to find out.

Networking in any entrepreneurial endeavour can never be emphasised enough. There will be people from all walks of life, working at all levels and you will need them in one way or another. So be wise and patient in interacting with them. Allowing people to win your trust with time will make for lasting partnerships. Similarly, working your way to win their trust will also win you lasting loyalties. Strengthen your network, not just to milk benefits out of it, but for a sustainable and holistic business development that can profit everyone. Do not be in a rush or greed to link arms with those that may seem powerful. You never know when you may be building caves for your own enemies to plunder into. Most importantly, learn to appreciate and encourage the underdogs and associates, even at junior level. They are the ones doing the real ground work for you and will show you the truest acknowledgement and return with the easiest investment of time, money or sentiments.

4

Better and Worse

They say that to build an empire is a battle, but to maintain the empire is the bigger endeavour. One can certainly assess one's strengths and weaknesses and work in their best capacity, with all factors built on the home ground. However, once the home ground is ready for the outside world and exposed to its opportunities and challenges is when the real struggle begins; one that put the foundation to test, one that brings up unpredicted, unprecedented developments and one that can make or break the future of the home ground.

The world of entrepreneurial kingdoms works on the same principles as well. Having evaluated his true strength and weakness – which included good subject knowledge, understanding of the market, good audience connect on the one hand, and low business acumen, weak negotiating skills and being new to this market, on the other – and addressing them to the best of his abilities, Ram had managed to set his footings in the business sphere of Chitrakoot. He had established himself as an amicable, ethical and efficient runner of a collaborative business platform in the name of Kutumb, functioning as a co-working space for small and large scale entrepreneurs across the whole spectrum of diverse professions.

The last four years had been a pendulum of extremes, with highs and lows for Ram, Sita and Lakshman. They had tried to carve ways for the new city to understand them, accept them and absorb them. But now, it felt like the struggle was over. With a series of struggles and a lot of collaborations, Kutumb had caught on magnificently. Ram had partnered up with some of the oldest stalwarts of the city and had managed to build an army of efficient and loyal employees. It was going well. It was perhaps going too well for everyone's comfort.

Complacence is a state that inertia pushes you towards. As an athlete, your ranking may make you complacent; as a student, your grade can do that for you. It is easy to specially become content when you have become the best at what you do in comparison to everyone around you. Ram was no super human and basic tendencies were quick to catch on to him too.

"Relax, will you? We will get it done in due time." He was speaking to Lakshman who brought forward an exciting opportunity for branching out in the neighbouring states.

"Word of Kutumb is out, Ram, and more people are realising that a collaborative, co-working space will make an excellent opportunity to expand businesses in B-towns. If we don't act now, we will soon lose the edge of the pace we have over people who may as well have started incubating their ideas for co-working spaces!" Lakshman was visibly worried. With local media coverage and a couple of awards, Kutumb had come into sufficient limelight. And yet, it had not gained the market popularity at such a scale that would bring it the market autonomy.

"For the business to thrive, we have to stay on our feet, keep coming up with ideas for in-depth expertise of innovation, as well as resources for horizontal expansion of the area," Sita seconded Lakshman. She had not been satisfied with the way things were going on at Kutumb and was getting bored and tired of the lack of challenges that had once encouraged her to dive nose first into the organization's mission. That was one of the most typical things about the trio. They often got together to brainstorm and discuss the pros and cons of their developments; they did so quite openly and honestly.

"Keep your critics close," was an ancient saying Ram sincerely believed in. His closest allies were his best critics, a blessing in disguise for sure! "You are right. Getting absorbed into the routine can be a huge mistake. We have to prioritize what's important and be constantly vary of what looks too good." Ram had spoken candidly, "I cannot forget what over-commitment on Dad's front led to… we practically had to give up our office because he did not realise when his assets turned into liabilities and got us into a huge debt with Kaikeyi. We clearly lost our sense of priority there!" Ram knew he could not afford to forget about these things.

Lakshman could not agree more, and in fact, had been meaning to point it out to his brother, "It is time for an honest review and discussion, especially with the ground staff, to understand where the real standing is and what needs to be revisited." In agreement, Ram decided it was time he sent his eyes and hands out in the field for some ground analysis.

Sita was out on a quality assessment trip with some interns. She saw some new signs up for advertisements for overseas opportunity. "Do you know what these signs are about? The one with the golden deer like logo?" She asked one of the interns curiously.

"Oh yeah, this new brand has come up recently. I don't know who is behind the scenes yet, but they are called the Head Hunters and collaborate with freelance skilled professionals and take them abroad on consultancy based assignments." The intern seemed to have heard quite a bit about the startup. Sita pondered, looking at the shimmering deer sign, a part of her mind piqued with inquisition.

"Are they any good?" she probed further.

"I don't even know, honestly. They're quite hush-hush about their identity. I am surprised I even spotted a logo so out in the open!" Now this was far too much for Sita to sit quietly on. She did not say a word there, but went home to do her research on the Head Hunters.

"I am telling you, Ram, these guys are on to something big. It is a fantastic business model, they have a very exclusive pool of resources and from what I can tell, the opportunity is very adventurous and diverse. We should definitely explore this opportunity!" Sita was all over the Head Hunters trumpet the next day at work. It was almost like her sense of complacence had been knocked out and the golden deer was teasing her.

"Okay, it is an opportunity worth exploring for collaboration. I will look into it," Ram finally gave in, in the face of Sita's persistent persuasion. He did not personally see a point in diversifying at this stage. They were doing pretty well with Kutumb's current model, as it is. "Let's set up a meeting with the Head Hunters, Lakshman… see if this is anything we'll like…"

And yet, some time passed without any action on either Ram's or Laksham's end to pursue the meeting. Sita reminded them a couple of times, but that did not translate into any results. Before long, her dissatisfaction had reached to a level of frustration and got her digging deeper into the whole golden deer chase.

What she did not realise was that every time she logged into the Head Hunters' website, setting up her registration ID for easy access, she was allowing phishing opportunities to many agents. "I know Lakshman had set up these firewalls for our own cyber security, but there's only so much risk in checking out the competition, right?" Sita thought to herself as she signed herself up for a form to file a request for a short term assignment. "I will not know what they do until I figure out a way to sneak into their model," she rationalised, without even realising who she was signing up for. With a determination to find new avenues for Kutumb and to tap on unexplored markets overseas, she applied for an Operations project. With all consumer details provided by Sita, the Head Hunters pitched to Sita for a project in Lanka, under the banner of another organisation, with clients she had worked with and an environment she could not refuse. With the intention to explore her chances of business expansion for Kutumb, Sita set off, finally lured by the golden deer!

Internal security is a huge risk in fast-rising companies. However, this is one of the most underrated investments that most bosses forget about. While entrepreneurs invest in security against external attacks, they forget that their most vulnerable asset is their human resource. Sita was a valuable person, both personally and professionally for Ram. However, with slight manipulations of regulations, Head Hunters had managed to attack Kutumb's system with malware and take enough data from Sita's forms to lure her out of the security zone.

"I understand that she needed an exploration, but she does not understand that this curiosity for looking at a new opportunity will have her trapped!" Lakshman thought. But there was not a lot to do except wait for Sita to figure out what she was after.

Several months had passed. Sita was making her own way with the Head Hunters and building a business opportunity for Kutumb to collaborate with. While in Lanka, Sita kept in touch with Ram through encrypted communication, passing on scopes and developments at the Head Hunters that could help them figure out a collaboration plan. What made matters more interesting, at least in the beginning, was that the Kutumb family also got interested in this affair and Ram began spending a considerable amount of time and resources in the pursuit.

"This would require a considerable amount of diversifying, Ram. Not to mention the whole investment that you will need to make to come up with the infrastructure to support it." Sugriva was genuinely concerned about the sudden shift of focus of Kutumb, especially at this critical stage of development, when bootstrapping had caused for resources to be minimal. There were a lot of things at play here. Kutumb was no longer a small experiment. It had become an enterprise with stakeholders, capital investments and really sensitive information that could change games. Everything said and done, high levels of protocols and security systems need to be maintained when such are the stakes involved. While Ram and Lakshman were cautious about their information going out, they did not bother enough to make sure that the team was built and held strong enough for a sustainable protection against breach! The business space they were working in, connecting online was the spine of all functionalities. But what Ram failed to pay attention to was the sheer number of people and therefore their devices that were vulnerable to cyber threats of data leak. Before long, there were enquiries coming in from Head Hunters, enquiries that looked and sounded promising, enquiries that could lead to solid overseas tie-ups, helping entrepreneurs find a base in the name of Kutumb, across borders. And Ram went on falling deeper and deeper into its trap, of bringing the enterprise into a vulnerable position.

Meanwhile, on a piece of land, far away, the stalwart behind Head Hunters had his own agenda going. Ravan, an unpopular business tycoon, was known for his ravenous stealth and queasy morals. Ravan was always on a lookout for fast-rising entrepreneurs and innovative business ideas to poach from, steal, or completely overtake business after running them hollow or ineffective. For this, he did not leave any stone unturned or any principle unbroken. As long as the price was right, Ravan found a way to break the wind.

"What is this name I keep hearing in India of late?" He had asked his business advisor, Shrupanakha after a quick tour back from India some years ago.

"Oh, Ravan, it is this fabulous idea I have been tracking. The guy seems to be a tasteful entrepreneur with a fair share of experience under his belt. But I don't think it will be very difficult to break him. I have heard that he is very gullible!" Shrupanakha said shrewdly. It was then that Ravan turned his full attention towards Kutumb and began employing different means to attract the enterprise's attention to find a way in.

However, things had not turned out the way he would have liked them to be. "Ram and his brother Lakshman, are both judicious and clever, Ravan," Shrupanakha had come back disappointed after a quest to get on the inside of Kutumb. Her attempts to lure them into an opportunity of partnership had not borne any results; clearly, bigger plans were needed.

Having found enough proof that Kutumb would be a promising business acquisition and explored the possibility of a direct approach, Ravan then set his malicious traps down. He began the advertisements of the golden deer, specifically in the city of Chitrakoot. "Make sure the word for Head Hunters is not out like a loose flyer. It has to be pictured as elite and exclusive; one that is not seeking, but that which should be sought." Ravan had instructed his team as his 'hunters' set out to execute his plan.

With time, Sita had taken the bait and given Ravan the much-awaited entry he was looking for into Kutumb, as well as into Ram's consciousness.

"Confidence can be a terrible thing, Shrupanakha," Ravan had relished Ram's vulnerability and predictability. It had been almost funny for him to watch the Kutumb team divide up and scatter all around, losing their focus.

He was not that far from the truth, as a matter of fact. It was Ram's confidence in his expertise and his position with regards to where he had brought Kutumb in the last few years of hard work that had brought him far closer to trouble than he could imagine. Perhaps because of his betrayal in Ayodhya, Ram had learned a valuable lesson. This lesson made him vary of others, vary of people taking advantage of him and his niceties. This had helped him evade quite a few challenges that came his way in these years. Establishing himself in Chitrakoot, winning over the hearts of people who barely knew him at all and finding loyalty and association with people of influence were all because of his judiciousness. And yet, Ram had forgotten one of the most important things to remember. Lost amidst the outside world, with friends and strangers, he had forgotten to pay attention to his own actions and look at where his focus was. His own confidence had begun to become a cause for his problems. The worst part was that he was not even aware that he was losing focus and chasing after a mirage that would lead him deeper into this loss and let other people take advantage of the situation.

While the mastermind far away was plotting to take advantage of Ram's disorientation, his team members, right under his nose, were experiencing their own challenges with the whole fiasco. There was looming dissatisfaction, lack of trust and rising rumours high and low in the Kutumb family, all within Ram's reach… if only he were willing to pay attention. Sita had been the first to be affected by this wave of dissatisfaction. Although it was true that she was the first one to fall for the allusion of the Head Hunters, it was clearly because of the lack of challenge and opportunity she had been feeling all along!

"Ram does not realise now, but all these years away from our history and Ayodhya's bitter experience has made him forget why we set our foot off that place," she would often think to herself, especially after a long and pointless discussion with Ram about how she felt they should be working on diversifying and expanding Kutumb's business model. Although Lakshman supported her ideas, Ram did not bother to get out of his complacence.

" Why does he always need a crisis to learn a lesson?" Sita could barely contain her frustration. "His understanding of his business aspiration is not in sync with the others on his team and this will lead him to a lot of trouble later, if he does not turn inwards and evaluate what kind of an erroneous omission he is making right now." Sita had had several of these discussions with Lakshman, who could well understand her angst.

It did not come as a big surprise to him then, when Sita took off to explore the Head Hunters' project offers, with her own idea of possible collaboration with Kutumb. What he did not contemplate, however, was the rising dissatisfaction that was biting others in the team too and would soon cause an uprising for Ram to tackle. It would not be long before people he thought he was counting on the most would start distancing themselves from him and destabilise the consistency, efficiency, quality and integrity of the team. This was going to turn out to be a hazardous mistake on Ram's part because even though he did not realize it, he was headed for quite a head-on catastrophe. In this time of need, he would really need the people he could bank on to stand by him and give their best shot to make sure that Kutumb did not sink. Ram was headed for a terrible shock, for when the people he had ignored under the shroud of his confidence would have burnt out, they would be unwilling to go the extra mile for him, because of all the distances that had creeped in between. Lost in his wild deer chase, Ram did not see any of that coming…

An entrepreneur is the vision designer of his business. It is their job to stay on the edge of their seat and keep their eyes, ears and mind open to all forms of growth, whether malignant, or benign. If complacence steps into the picture, even a flourishing enterprise becomes vulnerable to prying challenges. It is quite a compromising position to be in, since this vulnerability also opens up scope for dissatisfaction within the team. A true and efficient leader will be able to read into the early signs of unrest and figure out a way to either address the symptoms or work on the primary issue itself. If these elements of building chaos are not taken care of, it is possible to cause a threat to security and stability breach. An organisation that has not focussed on its members to win their consistent loyalty, nor given them an audience for expression of growth, will be susceptible to loss of important resources, be it in any form.

5

Culture is Key

"But Ram, why can't we get someone like Shrupanakha onboard?" Hanuman had asked several times. "She fits the criteria perfectly, is interested and willing to invest in our venture, and above all, you can't possibly ignore that she has the capital we need right now. We do not exactly have a whole line of funding agencies dying to give us money, in case you have not noticed!"

This was not the first time Ram had refused to work with someone who seemed perfectly fit and eligible for the needs of Kutumb. Despite their need for funding, however, Ram had made decisions that had alarmed everyone in the organisation.

"You do not see him in light of the bigger picture, Hanuman," Jamba, Ram's senior-most advisor on board, explained to the team. Jamba had been like a father figure to Ram and used to teach at Ram's college long before the young entrepreneur had passed out of the institution. They shared a much revered bond of mutual appreciation and Ram always sought Jamba's help. Once Kutumb had kicked off, Jamba had been kind enough to offer his assistance as a senior advisor on the co-sharing space's board. While Jamba never jumped into the driving seat himself, he would silently watch and observe Ram's work and that of the people around him. He would meet Ram often and discuss his decisions, flagging his mistakes wherever necessary and appreciating his achievements to encourage confidence in him. This relationship helped Ram to fight through his struggles and always gave him the strength in knowing that there is someone he could count on, for every step he took.

Even as everyone had been doubting Ram's decision making and assumed inexperience when he made decisions they did not understand, Jamba silently smiled and praised his student. "You have to understand that what appears at the surface is just the image people want you to see. Building an organisation is like building a house. You do not want it to just look good, but also to be strong and efficient." Jamba had been referring to the decision of not involving Bali in the business, contrary to everyone's expectations.

"What kind of people you bring into the organisation will determine what shades and moods your enterprise reflects," he explained to the interns during one of his all-hands sessions with them. Jamba went on to talk about the significance of establishing a culture when building an organisation, to make sure there is a sense of synchronisation and that every person is on-board with the same sense of purpose. "Otherwise, you are just a bunch of individuals drawing checks from the same account and working within a hand's reach from one another." Several heads nodded in agreement.

Team building was something Jamba had always stressed on with Ram, especially to bring a semblance between people from all walks of skills, with all kinds of experience. "Why do you think Ram takes these walks with all of you, spending one-on-one time with every level of worker?" That made many people smile.

"It is to connect with us," Hanuman answered with a beaming smile. He had had the opportunity of spending a lot of time with Ram in several meetings and felt special receiving this kind of proximity. When he looked around, almost everyone in that room had the same, grateful smile on their faces. As their leader, Ram made sure that everyone felt special, appreciated and respected. That was the kind of culture he wanted to spread amidst all the members of the Kutumb family, irrespective of their job title. It was becoming more and more obvious to the team now. Ram took all the efforts with everyone on his team so that they could build a bond. If the team had a good bond, there would be loyalty. If there was uniform loyalty, there would be undeniable trust. "And if there is trust, the organisation will stand strong, no matter what." The interns murmured, it all made perfect sense. You had to have the right kind of people working with you if you wanted to establish your footing as a strong and united organisation.

"And therefore, hiring the right people is a very critical move to this end. Hiring people just because they look right can be disastrous. It is very critical to see whether the person matches culturally with what you want your organisation to be like." Jamba summed up the thought that was probably already building in everyone's mind by now.

Keeping the bigger picture in mind, then, the team at Kutumb resumed their work to accommodate things they could not understand, or accept situations they could not comprehend. It did make some things a little complicated, but everyone had faith that Ram had their best interest in mind. "He will take care of things for us," is what was often heard echoing amidst the juniors when they faced any challenge. But it would be a great folly to think that everything continued as merry as a festival. There were things that did begin to trouble people, despite all their motivations and rewards.

One such dilemma was going on in the mind of Sugriva, one of Ram's first hires at Kutumb. He never let his troubles come in the way of his work, but he had a forlorn look on his face sometimes, and would have been noticed by anyone who was looking closely. As it turned out, Jamba was looking closely enough. "Sugriva, just because you feel grateful and loyal towards Ram, it does not mean that you speaking up about how you feel is going to be a bad thing. A loyal friend or employee is not one who agrees with everything that his friend tells him. On the contrary, if you are a loyal person, your dharma would be to show your friend where they are messing up or, as in your case, forgetting their promises," Jamba looked knowingly at Sugriva, understanding very well what had been upsetting the man. He gently nudged him to think about it and act upon it, not only in the interest of his own well-being, but also in the interest of his relation with Ram, which was now being affected.

It was this encouragement from Jamba that led Sugriva to finally ask Ram to go for a walk with him. “When you brought me on-board, I thought I have finally found someone who understands and respects me and will stand by his word… something that I take very seriously,” Sugriva began speaking to Ram with an open heart and mind. It was as though words were reaching Ram's ears before Sugriva could even utter them from his mouth. His expressions changed as the sudden realisation dawned upon him. When Ram had first brought Sugriva on-board, with his entire team of consultants, he had promised that Sugriva would be able to work in Kishkindha again, from the same office space he had bought many years ago with his life's savings. Bali had betrayed Sugirva and ousted him from his own property, rendering him and several of his employees jobless.

“You had looked me in the eye and told me that you see me for who I am and that you will help me restore the lost respect and value I once had…” Sugriva spoke to Ram in a soft, throaty voice. He had obviously been deeply affected by his brother's betrayal and still felt the pain.

Ram could not believe how big a fool he had been in forgetting something that had been so important. “I am so sorry, Sugriva. You have been like a brother to me. You came to join hands with me when I had nobody else to turn to. You had faith in me when I had nothing in my name. I should have respected your commitment and payed my due by bringing to you what is rightfully yours.” Ram was teary-eyed just thinking about the time when Sugriva had welcomed him with open arms and offered his help and the help of his entire team of consultants when Ram had barely anything to give him in return. There had been an unsaid bond of trust and respect between the duo. "I got lost in my mission to establish Kutumb and to bring it to a position of sustainability. When that happened, I got lost in the battle to elevate it above all other businesses and to beat any competition we were about to face. Amidst all of these battles, I forgot what my promises are, where my loyalties should be exercised first. These are no excuses for the mistake I have made. And I am humbled that you chose to remind me of what I have forgotten." Ram's words were enough for Sugriva to know he was with the right person and that his faith and loyalty had not gone to waste.

One of the most rare and priceless qualities in a leader is their humility. When an entrepreneur finds the strength and insight to identify their mistake and admit that they have erred, they have already established themselves above all the petty naiveties and set themselves on a path that will bring them closer to their ideology and their people. Ram may have erred in not remembering what promises he had made, but his admission of the mistake and assurance to correct it had been enough for Sugriva, and consequently his team, to find it in their hearts the forgiveness for their leader. As Ram entered his office back from the walk, he knew he had several errors to correct, and immediately picked up his phone, speaking to his real estate agent, asking for acquiring the biggest and most controversial property of Kishkindha. He was ready to pay any price for this victory.

Within the next month, the Kutumb family was being asked to prepare for a change. Nobody knew what it was, but Lakshman had asked the interns to prepare for some sort of compromises. “It is going to be a huge change. Some of you might have to go back to the way before we knew you…,” Lakshman's words were really beginning to scare the junior-most team.

“Hanuman, what do you think is happening, man? Is there some kind of a downsizing happening? Should we be worried?” The interns were asking all sorts of questions. Hanuman was the closest to Ram and if there was anyone who would have the answers, it had to be Hanuman. The young man, however, had no clue whatsoever. A lot of developments had been going on in a hushed up manner in the boardroom meetings. Hanuman was not a part of these discussions, though. He only knew one thing and that was the fact that he would trust Ram, come what may.

“Why do you worry so much? Have you felt in all these years that Ram has done anything to cause us any harm or affect us in any adverse way? He has always been sensitive towards how his team is doing and I am sure all his actions will ensure the right things for us.” Hanuman's words of blind faith sounded reassuring, but there was still a lot of mystery that needed to be resolved.

As the day of the announcement came, the team assembled in the conference room, with most juniors nervous to their wit's ends. The seniors, however, felt either confident or in the least, indifferent. A wave of silence fell over the apprehensive murmurs when Ram stepped into the room and greeted everyone with a sombre smile.

"Dear friends. You have known for a while now that Kutumb has been preparing for some changes. I have to say, this is not what I had imagined we would be doing just last month. But I have made a terrible mistake, and now, I don't have a choice but to do whatever best I can do to make amends." Ram took a pause, looking at everyone's face. Slowly uncovering the veils from over a giant structure that lay ahead of him, at the conference table, he slowly changed his serious face into a rising smile. "I present before you, the newly-acquired office space of Kishkindha!!!"

The seniors who had all known about the plan broke into a series of applause, hailing and shouting praises for the office model. The stunned, spellbound interns could barely breathe, taking in the model of their previous office sitting before them, with its structure and elements all held intact. The sign at the head of the layout read 'Office, Kishkindha Kutumb'. A closer look revealed a name label of Sugriva as the president of the new branch. As the truth of the revelation sank in, the hall erupted into a range of emotions, from laughter to tears, from people hugging each other to rushing to Sugriva and Ram to shake their hands.

"I told you... our faith will keep us going." Hanuman was nodding and shaking hands, speaking to anyone who could hear him. Wiping his eyes alongside, he did heave a sigh of relief. His leader had never disappointed him before, and it turned out, he planned on never doing that at all.

Jamba caught Ram in a silent corner as the entire team turned their attention towards the celebratory meal. Ram had a calm and humble smile on his face, one that revealed a lot of relief and joy and one that could only come as a feeling of gratitude. "You have done well, Ram. I know this bargain did not come easy to you. But this is one of the best decisions you have made ever since conceptualising Kutumb… and bringing me on-board, of course!" Jamba patted Ram lovingly on his shoulder and walked away to celebrate with the young team that was breaking into a dance at their own rhythm.

As Ram turned, he saw an emotional Sugriva approach him, steering him away from the crowd's earshot. "I am sorry I ever doubted your intentions towards me, Ram," Sugriva spoke, barely keeping his emotions in check as he felt a wave of gratitude drowning him. Ram did not need these words to have him realise how deeply Sugriva had been affected by this whole journey of ups and downs and how, his respect and faith restored, had set Ram in godly heights in his eyes. "I will have you know that my team and I are pledged now, more than ever, to work with you with the best of our abilities. Kishkindha will always be your second home now, and everything you have done for us, to restore us our home, our families and our lost respect, will not be forgotten."

There were many emotions that Sugriva was feeling as he shook Ram's hands. What he did not realise was that as Ram pulled him into a hug, there was another wave of emotions that Ram was experiencing himself. Having lost himself in the wild chase of victory, Ram had forgotten what Kutumb was really made of and that all the people who had been standing beside him while he had been building his enterprise from scratch, had slowly begun to be distanced from his proximity as he blindly continued to pursue his chase for success. It was when Sugriva had reached out to him and reminded him of his team that Ram had understood the loss he had been incurring by ignoring the happiness and well-being of his employees.

"It is possible that I am the one who comes across as the good guy and the hero in all of this, but I really was the bad guy who was reminded of the essentials by his good friend. That's what saved me from falling into a disastrous ditch," Ram spoke candidly with Lakshman as the two sat down for dinner much later. "Not only would I have left a critical promise unfulfilled and left several of my hardworking employees unsatisfied, but speaking from a professional and entrepreneurial point of view, this would have been a recipe for disaster. The people I was banking on the most for their loyalty were actually so troubled that they were beginning to get brittle with disappointment. If anything, this would have come to bite me when I wasn't even looking." Ram was lost in his own thoughts and was speaking to Lakshman about his most honest realisation when his brother turned his head to look at a middle-aged, sharp looking gentleman walk into the hall, seeming lost and yet determined. As he spotted Ram in the corner, he began striding towards him with firm, mediated steps.

The enterprise that you build is not just about the profits you make or the scale of your fame and achievements. At the end of the day, the success of your business is determined by the number of people who can connect with your enterprise and be positively affected by it. Investing your energy and synergy into building a healthy culture for your organisation is one of the most fundamental and yet, often ignored keys to sustainable development. A just and intelligent investment into building your team is a long term return plan. Watching for the right kind of people to hire and ensuring that the people who are hired are then kept satisfied is of utmost importance. As a leader, it is critical to keep track of your goals, but also to remember that you will not be able to reach that goal alone. In the process of development, making promises is natural. What needs special efforts is in making sure that the promises made are kept. This not only helps to restore the faith of your team, but also helps to build a culture of integrity and not just a transactional machinery, without any involvement or passion. It is critical that employees feel the transparent flow of information and can find themselves comfortable in reaching out to their juniors and seniors for anything. If there is this commanded freedom and openness, there is very little chance for miscommunication too.

6

Making Allies and Acquisitions

That sharp looking man had just walked into the Kutumb office and was working his way up to meeting Ram. There were many apprehensions, fear, even a hint of guilt and doubt because many would call him a traitor. But with his mind made up, Vibhishan waited patiently at the reception desk, waiting to be called in by Ram after having sent his card in. In these moments of anxiety, he thought back to his home, Lanka and his brother, Ravan and all that had transpired between the siblings that had led to such a dramatic trail of events.

They say a person is known by the company they keep. That is true at so many levels, but still remains one of the most understated learnings – in the professional domain, just as much as in the personal life. Associations and allies formed in one's life come to help you in all forms and situations, while enemies or dissociations can lead to a lot of damage in the long run. In the world of enterprises, a similar idea works.

Ram was immensely aware of the allies that supported his cause and enemies that hovered over his business like predators. "It is very important to understand who you are walking with, Ram," his mother had often told him as his friend and advisor. "Not everyone who smiles at you is a friend and not everyone with a frowning face is going to be an enemy!" Back in the day, when he was still training to be a rising entrepreneur, Ram had started watching for these markers in people to know how their association would turn out in the future. It is with this caution and training that Ram had established himself in Chitrakoot, carefully picking his friends and colleagues. Examples of lasting loyalty through Sugriva and Hanuman stood on one side, while deliberate distancing from potential harm presented itself through the examples of Shrupanakha and Bali. Ram understood the nuts and bolts of team building and brought his team together through skilful manoeuvring between rejections and selections.

While Shabri, a mere office assistant, had been willing to submit all her resources for the service of Ram, the senior most advisor, Jamba, had left behind his cushioned life to come and join his team out of sheer respect and loyalty for the man. "This is the kind of investment you need to make, as a leader. No fancy perks or job titles, no beating around the bush, but simple and honest empathy with your team members, an earnest respect for their situation and intellect, along with meaningful support to the extent possible," Jamba would often talk to Ram, Lakshman and Sugriva. "You will not see it in a day, but soon enough, you will have an army ready and waiting at your beck and call, with performance and efficiency far stronger than you could have expected."

As Kutumb went on to establish its branches in different areas, there was still the looming threat of Head Hunters that had been poaching their database and trying to lure more employees into switching sides. Sita had not really been poached successfully, but it was true that she had gone over for a Head Hunters assignment to Lanka, albeit with hopes of forming a healthy collaboration between the two organisations, but barely realising what Ravan was trying to take the situation over to his own advantage.

"I have dominated the land of Lanka for decades with my superior business skills and extraordinary leadership. There is absolutely no one who can supersede Head Hunters' shares in the market," Ravan boasted during one of his monologues as he addressed his senior management team. Like always, there was hardly any response or opinion that aired in the so-called brainstorming session. Despite being a strong team of able and experienced persons, no one really stood up to voice even an opinion, let alone a contradiction when it came to discussions with Ravan, who held the arrogance of ten heads over his shoulders! Initially, people did not contradict him out of fear of being dismissed or replaced. After all, Ravan was a rich and influential frontrunner of Lanka, who had almost monopolised over several businesses there. Over the years, it had almost become a culture of Head Hunters to simply comply with his whims, not so much out of fear now, but out of sheer complacence. It was as though Ravan did all the brainstorming on his own and autocratically announced decisions that were rash, erratic and often unethical. It was not far from the truth to say that Ravan believed he was the king of his empire and everybody under him worshipped him like a god. They did follow his orders, to be fair, but mostly for the lack of a better choice and even that seemed to be changing slowly.

"I don't understand how you all can sit and watch him play around with the law like this!" A young man was storming around on the terrace of the regal mansion where Ravan's family lived. Vibhishan, Ravan's younger brother, was a very intelligent and efficient manager. He had been Ravan's right hand for a long time, until he started seeing the flaws in Ravan's operation style up close and personal.

"Perhaps you are a little too attached to this than you need to be," Kumbhakarna, Ravan's other brother tried to reason with Vibhishan. "There are many things that go on in the background of business that you do not understand. Everything cannot be done with a white collar, brother!" Kumbhakarna was referring to the new deal that Head Hunters had signed by fixing the tender proposal they had submitted to the government. It had indeed helped Head Hunters grab a massive recruitment exclusivity for the government, but had hurt several smaller enterprises.

"If it had been just a one-time thing, I would still have accepted it in the name of the larger good, since we would be bringing jobs to so many people." Vibhishan continued to debate, "But he is taking commission for every single placement and it is only those who agree to this bribe that are going to be given jobs! That defeats the whole purpose of the employment generation programme."

His words fell on flat ears, though. Neither Kumbhakarna, nor his sister Shrupanakha wanted anything to do with a controversy against Ravan. Clearly, this was not the place to be wasting his energy. "I need to have a tough conversation about this with Ravan," he muttered to himself, walking away from his siblings.

An organisation can do great on certain parameters, like popularity, stock value or the number of clients. But whether or not it is being run by an enabling leadership decides how sustainable and fulfilling the business is going to be. Ravan may have become the richest businessman in Lanka, but he was certainly not the most popular one; least of all, in his own organisation. He was discriminatory, corrupt and apathetic towards his own team. There was nothing that stood between him and his lust for power, and for that, he was ready to cross all ethical boundaries. Vibhishan, on the other hand, may not have been the most ambitious entrepreneur, but he stuck by his values. This was something that often got him at odds with his own brother.

"But Ravan, you promised the staff you would give them a bonus if they worked overtime. You can't just change the numbers now and give them a false impression!" These endless debates went on long between the two brothers.

"Vibhishan, I can't keep doing charity for every person in Lanka. I have a business to run, and profits to make. You call it poaching, but these people would not have joined me if it was not a luring offer for them too, right?" Ravan would be defending himself at some other front when Vibhishan accused him of tricking organisations into signing contracts with Head Hunters based on its projected market value. For him, Vibhishan was a perfect waste of time; not just because he did not let Ravan function with full flexibility, but also because he did not seem to understand his ambitions and match his 'superior' means.

"Ravan, I have tried to tell you repeatedly that it is not just a matter of my personal principles and your apparent lack or ethical boundaries. This is about the culture you are setting for the company and what kind of sustainability you envisage for Head Hunters. Frankly, I don't think such means will stay hidden for long. Eventually, you might just get black-listed and end up with no business at all!" Vibhishan tried convincing his brother with a desperation that was eating him up from inside. He was edging more and more towards making a decision about his association with Head Hunters, what with the latest false acquisition of resources.

Ravan had been aggressively poaching contacts off the database of other organisations, tricking honest employees in the name of possible mergers, partnerships, or even funding. He had been retrieving a lot of critical and fundamentally damaging information from people in this wake and using it to his own advantage in the competing market. What had really ticked off Vibhishan was Ravan's duping stunt of bringing in a new bench of talents from rising startups and then getting all of their database in the name of performance edge.

"Now look at what you have done with Sita, for instance. She thinks she is here, working on a project that may lead to setting a base for her startup here. We both know you are shadowing her for the business model and contacts she has built… to defeat Ram and his business that has come up as your strongest and most damaging competitors around!" This discussion could have gone on for a really long time, but this is not what Vibhishan had in mind. There was a clear cut difference in their approach and ideologies and it was time for somethings to change. "Ravan, I have tried to give it a lot of time and deliberation, and unfortunately, I do not think Lanka will work out for me. When we started with Head Hunters, I thought we would bring together some of the best talents around and work on building a pool of excellence. Now, it just seems to me like a facade that I want to get away from…"

If it would have been anyone else, they would probably have asked for their brother and partner to stay back and make things work. Ravan did not think that way. He was okay with Vibhishan leaving Lanka; in fact, he was quite happy about it. "One less pain in my neck to deal with, honestly!" he muttered more to himself than to Kumbhakarna, who had just updated him with the news that Vibhishan had packed his bags and left Lanka.

With his short-sightedness and eyes only for the end results, Ravan was so far removed from his own reality. It would take a big jolt for him to realise his failure. What he did not know was that Vibhishan was actually heading to meet his arch-enemy and this would be leading to a massive turn of fortune. As Vibhishan moved determinant towards Ram's head office in Chitrakoot, he knew he was heading for a big challenge. He had heard that the young entrepreneur was a smart and caring leader, who had his eyes on the bigger picture, and his feet on the ground.

"Would he really be willing to talk to me? We have, after all, duped his partner into working for us, and have been stealing data off his panel…" He mulled over these thoughts as he waited in the lobby of Kutumb's office, waiting to be given clearance to meet Ram. Another battle ensued in the background as Ram and Lakshman discussed and debated what to expect out of Vibhishan.

"But Ram, you know Vibhishan has been one of Ravan's closest associates. The Head Hunters have been infamous for breaking all ethical boundaries and this might as well be their latest stunt to take out the opposition." Lakshman was worried. Shrupanakha had been trying to convince them into tying up with Head Hunters for a while, and now, Vibhishan had showed up with a proposition. It all felt too sketchy to have faith in.

"There is no harm in talking to the man. Ravan may be a man without the strongest virtues, but I have run a background check on Vibhishan. He is a man of honour and it is believed that the brothers did not get along in principles. This could be a way of forming a great alliance." Ram contemplated, extremely aware of both sides of the arguments, knowing well that he would need to be careful about this and yet, the possibilities that await at the other end of this meeting.

He walked into the reception area, greeting Vibhishan with a smile. It was then that the two honourable men looked each other in the eyes and knew instantly that they were made of the same set of values.

"Ram, I tried my best to convince my brother to turn away from his treacherous methods, but he has power rushing up his head and does not realise what peril he is leading the organisation into. I have worked really hard for the people and the business. I don't want to see them go down like this. I am here because I have heard great things about you and I believe that you are a fair businessman. I have no hidden agenda here; I just want to help you in helping me in bringing the organisation under a just leadership." Vibhishan did not mince his words because he knew Ram would appreciate honesty. This is the only thing he had aspired for in his professional career, to be recognised for his work capacity and to be associated with someone he could sync with on the level of principles.

It is for this reason that often even the best of friends as well as relatives, especially siblings, fall apart in entrepreneurial partnerships. The criticality of this necessity is lost on many people, but the best in business understand that this is not just a matter of principles, but the only sustainable way for your business to have a strong future, to align it with people who have the same mission and vision as you, and that you look at both the means as well as the end you want to get to. Several people had questioned Ram's decision-making skills when he made unpredicted moves and brought on-board surprising partnerships. Agreeing to partner with Vibhishan, which he eventually did on the basis of his gut feeling and background check on Ravan's brother, Ram had taken a risk, but a calculated one. He knew he would be benefitting on many levels from not just getting grave insight into the strategies and working model of Head Hunters, but also because Vibhishan by himself was a great asset who would bring to the table a lot of experience and resources. In this way, Ram had succeeded in turning his competitor's weakness into his own strength and this strategic move was about to bring him a lot of advantage on big things and small, something that Ravan had completely chosen to look over, in his arrogance and blind drive for power.

The kind of allies you make, lose or are able to retain very strongly, reflect on both the culture and future you are building for your organisation. As an expanding entrepreneur, there will be several choices, many of which will hold great potential and simultaneous risk that may need to be evaluated before the choices are made. It is here that a lot of judiciousness, homework and experience comes in handy for a businessman. Gauging the strengths and weaknesses of your enemy is critical, since it helps you understand what you yourself may be doing right or wrong in the process. It is a very helpful and healthy habit to keep a close check on the environment you work in, analysing all the developments and trends that go around. Otherwise, you may just get stuck being on an island, blinded by what you presume to be your success, and never even realise what losses you may incur for yourself, both inside and out of the organisation.

7

Know Your Competition

"Now, what he generally does is that he makes the client feel the crisis and then offers Head Hunters as a solution. What the client does not know is that the assumed crisis is also a scenario designed by Ravan himself!" Vibhishan sat, explaining to Ram, Lakshman, Sugriva and Jamba in one of their early meetings. Over the last few months, he had been giving them a lot of insight about Head Hunters' approach and tactics for client acquisition, most of them bordering around unethical practices. Head Hunters' expeditious growth in the last few years had baffled the entire market. Their stock value was through the roof, the giants from across the world had made contractual agreements with them for exclusive hiring, while a huge section of their competitors had either succumbed to an aggressive merger or turned their business elsewhere as pitied peripherals.

"It may look really fancy and successful from a distance, but the real story behind Head Hunters is not a pleasant one. Ravan invests heavily in brand building, PR and advertising. But his staff is ridiculously underpaid, his facilities are only functioning precariously while there are so many rules he has flouted because of relations in the higher places, that it is almost dangerous to be associated with him. Of course, all of this is swept under the glamorous carpet and what people see is numbers and buildings under the Head Hunters' name." Vibhishan continued to unveil the actual skeleton of Kutumb's biggest enemy.

Sugriva and Hanuman exchanged glances every now and then, as though looking out for any signs of deceit from Vibhishan. He was, after all, from the enemy's camp and it would take a lot more than just a few warm words and hugs to melt the walls of these hard core warriors.

"Ram may have his belief system, and while I trust him completely, I cannot deny that he is too trusting and always looks for the good in people. I would like you to help me in keeping vigilance against Vibhishan, to make sure there is no damage we cannot reverse," Sugriva and Hanuman had discussed soon after Vibhishan had been brought on-board the Kutumb team. They would always instigate Ram to raise questions, despite his better judgement, and they were not going to stop until they were convinced.

"But how come there have been no investigations into all the fraudulent practices? Head Hunters has got to be under the radar for all its limelight. Has no one seen through it?" Hanuman asked perplexed with all the new information he was getting.

The idealist in Ram could not fathom such conniving tricks. "Oh Ram, there is a lot that can be turned by the power of money. People in the highest positions look for power while those lowest on the power ladder can easily be swayed by money." Jamba, sitting next to Ram, patted kindly on his shoulders, knowing well that this must be upsetting for the fair businessman.

"Exactly!" Vibhishan added, "All auditors are taken to luxury resorts, all policy makers are sent on exotic 'exposure trips' and the media is pretty much living out of Ravan's pocket. Any error reported is already being covered for, every mistake has a price tag."

It was all too shocking for Ram to imagine how someone could get to that level for success and still go undetected. Lakshman, the more practical of the two brothers, also felt that water was neck deep in this one! "I think we know now how Ravan has been stealing all our resources and expanding his business so fast. That will have to be addressed at a higher level of administration and governance," Lakshman had quickly come into brainstorming mode and was trying to pick all the threads to weave together solutions. "In the meanwhile, we have to get some intel on the potential clients they are about to hack," Lakshman said more to himself than to others around him.

Jamba, observing the brothers deliberating closely added his two-pence, "I think that is a great idea. It would be very helpful to send someone inside. Just like they sent Shrupanakha here, we should send someone there for getting more information about their client list and financial status." Jamba looked knowingly towards Hanuman, well aware of his eagerness to help Ram out and at the same time, assess the actual situation of Head Hunters and Lanka.

"While I am there, I'll probably try to get hold of Sita and ask her about her contract and work arrangements too. Maybe she has some insight that we do not know about." Ram had always admired Hanuman's eagerness to take on challenging tasks. Never hesitant or doubtful, Hanuman was always up for experiments and explorations. Ram always pushed him to explore his boundaries and capacity, knowing well that Hanuman always learned something out of the whole experience. Hanuman, on the other hand, always felt confident about pushing himself and following Ram's orders because his boss had, after all, proved his sincerity and well-meant strategies time and again, ensuring Hanuman that he had his back. Hanuman was eager to get on this experiment and figure out the market of unchartered territory with twice the excitement.

Lanka was a lot more than what Hanuman had expected. 'It really is all glamour,' he thought to himself as he stood in front of the Head Hunters building. It was a mammoth structure, oozing show and pomp. It was obvious that the entrance had been designed to create awe. However, Hanuman was not one to be fazed by its glitter. His agenda was to meet the staff, pitch his talent and return with as much data as possible. After having waited for quite some time, Hanuman finally found himself an audience with the senior leadership. While Ravan was not around, the other senior directors of Head Hunters had welcomed him for a discussion. After all, he was from Kutumb, the only threat that had arisen in the horizon of their market.

"I don't have any hidden agenda here, ladies and gentlemen," Hanuman started out humbly and clearly. "I would just like to see if there is any scope for Kutumb to get on-board with your projects. We are aware that the two organisations have come dangerously close to being arch-enemies. Ram, however, does not want this to head to a bitter storm. If there's a way to amicably strike a deal where we can both win each other's support and you can return our assets, there would be nothing Kutumb would like more than a friendly alliance." Hanuman looked deep into the eyes of his listeners, finding some smirking, others contemplating. It was obvious that the crowd held mixed opinions about Ravan's means of achieving success. But no one was going to blatantly support Ram's business in Lanka.

"I do not know what you were thinking when you came here, Hanuman," Kumbhakarna bellowed from his chair. "But Ravan is really specific about what he does with people who try to be diplomatic or even sly. You are too beneath his status to even be allowed to approach him directly." These were vain words of an arrogant leader, who thought he could throw his power in someone's face and demand their respect. Even as he spoke, there were staff members shaking their heads in disapproval, waiting for the whole embarrassment to end.

"I see why Head Hunters needs such a tall and flamboyant building to hide behind," Hanuman spoke, still with a gentle voice but a gaze that shone with pride of deeds. "At Kutumb, we let our actions speak for themselves, instead of shiny arrangements. And our leader inspires us towards excellence instead of arrogance, you see. That is why the peon and the CEO, all eat and walk together. I doubt that your leader would ever have demonstrated that culture here." Hanuman was fuming on the inside, but holding his dignity high, he walked out the board room quietly. On his way, he met an old friend who used to once work with him in Kishkindha but had moved out after Bali's taking over of the business. This meant there was going to be a lot of conversation over lunch!

"Everything said and done, Hanuman, this place is not worth applying to. We get called with a different set of roles and responsibilities, but as you start working here, these roles are slowly replaced with other tasks, mostly directed by Ravan himself. There is no space for growth, neither is it a lucrative arrangement, since Head Hunters keeps a huge cut from our contractual amount, in the name of on-boarding allowance." Hanuman's friend had been spilling out all the facts from behind the stage of this massive facade. "They charge the clients less than competing parties for tenders, since they have inside information on each of these. They are able to quote so less because they ask the clients to pay minimal basic salaries, while the rest is all evaded from tax slabs as allowance. To make matters worse, they give us a couple of extra projects on the same payroll, while charge companies extra in the name of exclusive resources. This goes on and on…"

Hanuman had gathered enough proof, in terms of clientele information and financial biddings that Head Hunters worked with. With all this information, he had enough backing to make a solid case with the government to blacklist Head Hunters. His next stop would be to find Sita and ask her to come back.

"This is how he manages to crack every deal here at such astonishingly low prices, Ram," Hanuman discussed with Ram over the phone after a couple of days in Lanka. He filled him in with all the details he had gathered about the corrupt organisation. Ravan's existing and targeted client list, his asset details, and even a document on his malpractices had reached Hanuman after calling in a lot of favours from the clerks who worked at the bottom of the pyramid.

"I will probably get into a lot of trouble if they found out. But I am sick of working under Ravan's autonomy. I do not feel the slightest bit respected or recognised after toiling for hours here." One of the finance clerks had opened up to Hanuman when he got to know he worked at Kutumb with Ram. "Head Hunters has amazing reviews on online job portals. But we know the truth… these portals have fake PR posts while the real feedback is buried under the hatchet. I have been hearing good things about Kutumb, but I also know these comments are authentic because I know Ram's background." This conversation led to a lot of revelation that Hanuman kept passing to Ram while still trying to talk to the business crowd in Lanka.

"I cannot go around snooping into all departments, looking for Sita. They will never grant me the access." He was being completely shut out by Head Hunters and all their existing clients.

"If you can't reach Sita, have her reach you. Kutumb holds a lot of brand value and this will really help you pass on information that can reach Sita out of sheer word of mouth." Ram had complete faith in Hanuman's capabilities and a clear idea about how the brand value of Kutumb worked in their favour. It was now time to put it to good use and show Lanka what a real brand looked like.

It is fairly simple to fall into the trap of false noise, especially in the scenario of an aggressive and competitive market space. What really needs to be focussed on is ground realities and facts. Instead of being intimidated by uncharted territories and mighty brand images, it will help to invest in market research, to assess the target audience as well as the competitors, to assess their products and services and know what people have to say about these products and services. It is not surprising that a lot of marketing insight can be achieved by simply peeking under the visible skin of the market. It is not advisable to take things on face value, irrespective of whether these impressions are good or bad. Once reality has been explored first hand, you will be in a better position, both fact-wise and confidence-wise, to pitch yourself against competition and surpass their standards. Making an unbiased competitive analysis makes you understand where you stand in the market positioning, what works for your market leaders and what is present there that is lacking on your side. Once such derivations are made, only then can you work on strategies to fill the gaps or gain an edge.

8

In the Name of Ram

The event was turning out to be a lot bigger than Hanuman had imagined it to be. Day after day, more and more registrations had been pouring in for the Grand Entrepreneurial Expo. With Ram's advice, Hanuman had set up a mammoth meet for rising entrepreneurs from India, as well as Lanka to all come together and put up their exhibitions. There were going to be stalwarts from all forms of businesses, as speakers as well as observers. "This will be serving several purposes for us, Hanuman. It is not just an expo to have Sita reach us, but also a strong statement for us to establish our presence in Lanka, to attract eyes of the government, the corporates, the competition and also educational organisations that will be sending in their teachers and students to the Expo for exposure." Jamba was explaining to Hanuman during one of their telephonic conversations.

When Hanuman had been unable to locate Sita during his visit to the Head Hunters' office, he had been rattled by the lack of options. "If I had been back home, I would have channelised all my sources to get in touch with her. But here, I feel like a fish out of water. I do not know what will work!" Hanuman had spoken to Ram and Lakshman about a month ago.

"Don't see this as a time of crisis, Hanu. This is your moment to bring forth the brand of Kutumb and show the world what we are made of," Ram had patiently advised his subordinate. It was simple calculation. Kutumb had been growing steadily in and around Chitrakoot, building a substantial market value and share in northern India and parts of southern regions too. All it took was a phone call or an email from Ram and people would come running for collaborations and initiations with Kutumb. His troop of alumni were as resourceful as they were loyal.

"That is the thing about keeping your community impact intact," Jamba was once talking to the interns. "The reason I am here, helping Ram, is because we share a bond of loyalty and integrity. The value of his Gurukul was not just in the education it gave him, which of course, has its own credit, but in the fact that it acts like a strong statement in itself."

Ram had maintained a healthy and honest relation with his batchmates, juniors, seniors and professors from Gurukul and had always turned to his community for help and guidance. "A lot of his allies come from Gurukul. People who have studied with Ram are well aware of his work efficiency and ethics and feel confident about working with him for their needs." This would prove to be true for several rising entrepreneurs of their times. There was the whole bunch of interns that came with Sugriva out of sheer following and community rapport. On the other hand, when Ram had been building Kutumb from scratch, many of his old friends and colleagues had helped raise crowd funding for the initial expenses. "The point being, you work on your reputation as a person, in every little action and word. Even when you do not have a brand yet, every bit is working towards building that brand. And that pays off later," Jamba had concluded his free-speech of the day. It was very true. People remembered Ram as the exemplary friend and leader, the ethical practitioner and the loyal associate who would do anything to prove true to his words and fulfil a commitment. It was this signature that helped Ram build an identity of Kutumb that was considered synonymous with him and brought it, by default, the same credibility as himself. Kutumb resonated with Ram's ethical commitment to service.

It was this brand identity that had helped Hanuman circulate information about the Expo in Lanka. People know people who know people. It was always possible to find contacts, reliable sources and allies when you are associated with a name that holds a brand value as powerful as Kutumb. Without going over the top, Hanuman began seeking presence of visitors for panel discussions, especially amidst the high ranking stakeholders of Lanka. He tried a couple of places by himself, not with much success though. He would be met with regretful faces of receptionists and assistants who had no idea what Kutumb was or what this foreigner was doing in their office. This, however, changed impressively when he started carrying out a methodological approach, with a pre-set buzz, amidst important media houses about the industry's largest Expo being organised. When Ram called in favours, with the help of Vibhishan, the government of Lanka could not turn down the offer to endorse the Expo and facilitate a smooth progress.

"This is going to be a great opportunity for small and large businesses to diversify and find viable options for their collaborative tasks. We all know that contractual market has been booming with a higher efficiency. And we do want our future businessmen, our MBA students, to ride the right trains, do we not?" Ram had tactfully questioned the spokesperson for ministry of financial affairs of Lanka. Once that head had nodded, it was not very difficult to find access to many business portals.

"Hanuman, you must now go in with this letter from the ministry, your branded bag, accessories and a gift hamper for every organisation. The logo of Kutumb is something that should be etched into their minds like the jingle of the Expo we have been airing on the radio," Lakshman expressed once all the branding material had been sent across to Hanuman's makeshift office in Lanka. This would mean a lot more impact and better brand recognition for Kutumb, making both accessibility and availability easier.

Hanuman, with his new equipped brand strategy, began advertising in a selective and filtered method, with indirect marketing, making space for word of mouth. "The Great Entrepreneurial Expo is not for everyone. It is a unique opportunity for businesses and independent entrepreneurs to expand their growth platform and to build a long term plan," Hanuman declared to one of the front runners of technology in Lanka. "What Kutumb is providing is a solid, practical and ethical plan for entrepreneurial growth." This, along with endorsement from the right people had begun to bring about a consistent buzz amidst business owners of the country, placing the stepping stones for the Expo.

As the days for the Expo neared, Hanuman received a call from an application that looked distinctly familiar and invited him for a meet-up. Although the invite came from the mother source of Head Hunters, it did not specify which collaborative wing it had originated from. Hanuman, deep in his heart, realised that he had found Sita; or rather, she had found him. He sent back a letter of acceptance, on the letterhead of Kutumb, with a humble home sign that the team within Kutumb used for their internal communications. Sita knew she had found the right person responsible for organising the Expo… it was her beloved Ram, with his eyes and hands in Lanka, in the form of Hanuman.

When they finally met, Hanuman was overjoyed to find his long gone friend. "Oh Hanuman, I have been dying to see your familiar face!" Sita was just as overwhelmed at this reunion. "It has been so hard for me to continue working in sync with Head Hunters, knowing very well where their interests lie and how they have been manipulating everything to get their business going." Sita had been working on a collaborated project with Head Hunters as her parent client and this had led to a lot of revelations. With time, she had earned the friendship and trust of several management level employees and found out as much as possible from the product managers of Head Hunters as could possibly reveal their weaknesses and strategy for expansion.

"There is so much we can do to get an edge over Ravan. Not only is there enough proof of illicit activities through its backdoor, there are such fundamental flaws in his management that it has ticked off most of his employees, who will be happy to work under another boss." Sita was excited to meet someone from Kutumb and share all the details of her discovery. With her phone and email communications tracked through the Head Hunters' server, it would have been impossible for her to send any information back home. But now, with Hanuman as her ally, she knew they could work categorically to outpace Ravan's tricks.

Back at the head office, Jamba sat with Ram and the whole team, deep in thought after the telephonic conversation he had just had with Hanuman. "Now, Ravan is aware that Kutumb is stepping into his territory. It will not be very difficult for him to trace the Expo back to us. However, Ravan's biggest flaw is his hubris. He is so arrogant about his power that he will not even know that we are working in front of his eyes and building an army." Ram was thinking strategically, in terms of taking the next steps. He had gotten a few emails from his contacts in and around Lanka, all suggesting the eagerness with which the business group was awaiting the stepping in of Kutumb.

"We have to start working on the identity of Kutumb and make it popular amidst the target audience. We will project a strong and uniform message, sent through multiple platforms. Let us reach out to the most established organisations, as well as the institutes churning out young professionals; we have to address both the old and the new." Ram quickly spoke his mind. The staff rolled into motion, picking up assignments. Hoardings, banners and invitation cards – all holding out the same theme of messages from Kutumb – were printed and placed throughout the campaign areas. Merchandise, cards, invites and hampers, all prepared with Kutumb's logo. The team went full swing on the marketing, with blogs, statements, press releases, and viral videos. The team of interns were sent along with Sugriva to set up base for the Expo.

As Hanuman waited eagerly for the team to arrive, he went on with his homework, meeting people, setting up themes for the Expo, rolling out registrations and giving talks at business institutes with the accessories. However, even hours after the scheduled arrival time, the team of new recruitments had not yet landed in the cyber city of Lanka.

"There is some mistake here. They are not letting in such a large group of unidentified people with so much equipment," Sugriva spoke to Hanuman over the phone. It had not struck Hanuman before, but this was bound to happen. They were treading in uncharted territories. They needed to resonate with Ram's reputation and identity to get things done. On Jamba's advice, Hanuman immediately got ID cards made for the interns. They all read 'Ram's Squad for Expo'. As soon as these IDs were handed to the interns, they were permitted clearance and poured into the cyber city with the entire entourage. Within days, entire Lanka was buzzing with the excitement of the Grand Entrepreneurial Expo. Guests pouring in from across the country and abroad, hotels being booked, registrations overwhelming for participation.

As the D-day approached, the team got ready for the inauguration. The prime minister of Lanka herself had agreed to honour the inauguration ceremony with her presence. This had not just been a lucky day; a lot of hard work had gone into building the reputation that had allowed for this achievement. Ram and Lakshman had been working on the foundation of this relationship for over a month. They had tapped into the weakness that Ravan had exposed – his lack of relationship building and trust with the government authorities. Ram had personally attended several meetings and sat with every single appointment to be done for resource allocations through the co-working space for his clients. Within the month, they had been able to deliver with such accuracy, that a unanimous reputation of reliability and quality had been found to have developed between Kutumb and all stakeholders. It was because of this crisis handling that the organisation had done for the decision makers of Lanka that the prime minister was standing with Ram, on the very first day of the Expo, and addressing the crowd with words of praises and expectations from such a platform.

The name of Ram, his institute and his service had helped build a brand value that was now not only being acknowledged, but also praised and sought for in a foreign land. Breaking the clutter of several service companies, Kutumb had built for itself a unique selling point of reliability and customised quality, based on the need of their client. This is what they had resonated with all their marketing strategy and every piece of advertising and other communications, making people think of Kutumb as a brand that commanded respect and trust, something they had specifically been missing in the market space of Lanka because of Ravan's indiscriminate and insensitive autocracy. It was the very first day of the Expo, but the potential was already promising. There was a lot more going to happen in the coming week during the duration of the event. Ram could already sense it.

A business may have all the right qualities that are needed by a client, but this will not be seen or even detected unless there is an effective branding done to project the same. In a market full of options, aggressive competition and clutter, there has to be a unique selling point that needs to be projected and exploited for the clients to take notice of you, to even consider you as an option. For projecting a unique selling point, it will bring you a great strategic advantage if you assess the strengths and weaknesses of your competitors and then pitch for a unique selling point that they have failed to offer. The connect with the client at a level that addresses their distress goes a long way and helps build your reputation as a reliable brand. This may seem like a lot of extra miles in short-term goals, sometimes even not so economically viable, but will serve a lot for the long term vision if practiced with the right strategy at the right time. It is important to keep a marketing message consistent and prominent for an effective brand recall and efficient user bandwidth.

9

Financial Sustainability

"How can this be happening to us?" Ravan bellowed in his office, surrounded by a team that looked both scared and disappointed with Ravan's rage, even more than the actual gravity of the situation. Ever since the inauguration of the Grand Entrepreneurial Expo, Lanka had been taken by a rage of influx from businesses across the globe. People from all spheres and geographies had come to attend, interact and build business opportunity on Kutumb's model of conglomerated resource management. This had suddenly put Lanka on a map of entrepreneurial opportunities.

"I cannot believe we have had such a large hub of talent and infrastructure waiting right under our noses and we have never tried to tap it," a reputed investor spoke on the podium during a panel discussion after declaring his intentions of investing the largest fund in the history of Lanka in campus placement of Lanka National University, all with the support of Kutumb. But in doing so, a lot of feathers had been ruffled, and a lot of hustling had rubbed business partners the wrong way. After all, it was not Ravan's forte to connect with people and think for the larger good. The power hungry, self-proclaimed leader had a unilateral and top-down approach in building up a business for himself. So, naturally, when Ram emerged as a promising option for the aspiring population of Lanka, it did not take very long for the long-awaited shift of loyalties to materialise.

"Ahiravan, I don't know where you are going to get the funds from, but I want Head Hunters to have the biggest possible exhibition at the Expo. We will get into Ram's own comfort zone and defeat him at his own game. Nobody gets away with pulling a stunt at me!" Ravan was infuriated and asked his brother to follow his commands to the T.

"But Ravan… that is what I am trying to tell you…" Ravan had already walked out of the office before the distraught sibling could even begin with a logical explanation for Ravan. "There are no funds… and our investors are turning cold feet, looking at the massively changing trend in the country towards Ram. Anyone funding us will be throwing themselves deliberately against the wind and also send a strong message of association with what the country is clearly opposing right now!" It seemed like Ravan had been digging his own grave with the shovel of his arrogance in the last decade. Financial management had clearly not been his strength.

It had all begun to show in the culture of Head Hunters when Ravan had gotten a deer of real gold made and installed at the doorstep of the building in what he declared to be a power play. However, most perceived it as a vulgar display of money and, in Vibhishan's words, an extravagant stunt to polish his self-importance. This was one of the most fundamental problems with Ravan's management policies.

Ever since the series A funding had fallen through, Ravan had become drunk with power and lack of foresight. "I want the world to know that it is glamorous to be associated with Head Hunters. Our clients should feel like they are royal… actually each and every move we make should breathe of royalty," he had declared a long time ago, while hiring a marketing agency to build the brand name of Head Hunters. One of the most basic mistakes made by rising entrepreneurs who have hit the right nerve is that they take on an impression of invincibility. While a strong sense of confidence is essential, there is also the threat of satiation that can overpower strategic steps and throw finances off the course.

"Ravan, as your well-wisher, and the well-wisher of Head Hunters, I just want you to reconsider our priorities," Vibhishan would always insist back in the day, when the brothers still saw eye to eye. "We have to prioritise our investments." Ravan and Kumbhakarna exchanged the typical eye-roll they always did when Vibhishan started talking.

"We can't all be the boring and drab businessmen that you want us to be, Vibhishan. We have enough funds to spend and it is not like we are doing this as a luxury. Building a brand is an important strategy to attract clients to associate with us." The brothers had justifications ready for the expenses they had incurred in the past or planned to exercise in the future.

Vibhishan, despite repeated rejections, was not one to stop from trying them to see the light of logic. "I am not asking you to be miserly, but a brand message of royalty is definitely not necessary. In fact, it can be quite misleading for organisations that might actually want to be associated with us, but are getting discouraged because of the elite brand consciousness we are bent on building for us." Vibhishan looked around for support in a conference room that was full of people trying to please Ravan, beyond the realm of logic or foresight. Despite bringing up this issue with several people individually, he was always met with disappointment.

"What could possibly go wrong with the golden deer?" They asked him. "It is associated with pride and helps with the publicity! We have enough funds to afford such PR activities," they would declare unabashed. Unlike the rational thinking of Vibhishan, theirs was clouded with the passion of glamour and power, notwithstanding the utter disapproval it earned from their VC, who could barely convince themselves about the way marketing was developing for Head Hunters. This, extended and exploited over the decade, had led not just venture capitalists but also clients to be put off with the Head Hunters' extravagant style of execution. While most were in search of pure and simple talent for project executions, Ravan was selling them an idea of building an impression, a facade, if you will. "For the world to see how accomplished you are," in Ravan's rhetoric. While this propaganda had been bought by many aspiring businesses in the beginning, eventually, they all came to realise that the high horse was not what they needed, at least, not all the time. With racing budget numbers and disproportionate input to output returns, it was quite obvious that most of the business owners in Lanka, who were on the receiving end of Ravan's bills, found themselves stuck in the rut of the trend that Ravan had built. It was high time someone did something to change that.

On the other hand, there were changes happening in small but significant ways, in the entrepreneurial growth, not so far away from Lanka. Kutumb had been setting quite an exemplary tone for a business model. Although not miserly, but financial managements were being taken very seriously.

"Our vision is to support and encourage small scale businessmen and independent talents to find a platform with large enterprises, to build a win-win situation for everyone. Profits come in scale, numbers, and above all, the impact that Kutumb has set forth to achieve," Ram would often discuss with his team. The culture and vision in the office was made clear time and again, with repeated and inclusive discussions with everyone.

While team Kutumb did not believe in frugality as a guiding principle, they did appreciate value for money and a focussed strategy. "As long as there is focus and realisation of the mission, there is no hesitation in expenditures that are due." Jamba often discussed with the product designers. However, wherever possible, several attempts were made to make sure that this bootstrapped organisation never shot above their affordability, without compromising the quality.

Sugriva and his team of young interns were a highly treasured resource for Kutumb. “It is not just because they are cheap, it is also because they are eager to learn, diverse and will eventually lead to forming a trail of efficient team members who are in alignment with the team's working principle and methodology,” Jamba reasoned with Lakshman, who advocated that going the intern way would not be an effective long-term strategy.

“We need a group of experienced and efficient talent. Otherwise, we will end up babysitting for a very long time and not know how to filter between what is good and what is excellent.” Lakshman would often refute.

Such a series of healthy discussions and disagreements were quite common between the core team of Kutumb. Not only was such a culture encouraged, but also triggered by organising what was called a 'hot box', where conflicting ideas and mindsets were put to brainstorming in their discussion forums. “This often leads to genius ideas that are well thought-out, resonating with resourcefulness and optimised efficiency. If the funds are unlimited and easy to find, there is little scope for scratching below the surface and coming up with what is beyond the ordinary,” Jamba picked on the team's brain often with such titillation.

During their quarterly financial planning, team of Kutumb had a simple strategy of looking at their worst case scenario and building backwards from there. Anyone who managed financial aspects of Kutumb – be it a project or the overall organisational management – was always in sync with the principles that guided the organisation. It was something that instilled overall ownership and accountability in the employees.

"The bottom-up approach is the way to go about it… let the people know they are the decision makers of financial management of their wings and let them face the consequences of their management. This will make them accept an ownership of the money spent while giving them the due agency to take decisions that they feel are viable," Jamba had discussed with Ram and Lakshman during a strategic meeting.

When this approach was rolled out, it brought revolutionary innovations in the team. While some were apprehensive of the responsibility, many took it like a leap of faith. When Hanuman was sent on the excursion visit to Lanka, he had the independence to manage all the resources on his own, to spend as per rationality and to engage in all attempts necessary to prepare for the ground work of the Expo.

"Come on, Hanuman, you have been curating the whole Expo for over a month now. I think you can deserve to rest for a while and allow yourself the treat of a vacation at the weekend. I am sure Ram won't mind. In fact, he might not even notice this little treat amidst the massive expense sheet you have been sending back in the preparation phase," Surasa, one of Hanuman's several associates in Lanka had tried to lure the devoted man once. It was common in the Lanka business culture to entertain business associates and engage in what was called 'social development'.

Spending on non-work related activities in the name of business development and client acquisition was quite the trend. Therefore, when Hanuman turned down this offer by Surasa, this was a strong message about the honesty and integrity of Hanuman. It also etched strongly that business-focussed objective of the employee, and in extension, of the culture inculcated in Ram's organisation.

It was not the only time when Kutumb had extended due diligence in financial humility. Several of their clients were in awe with how much respect and emphasis was laid on resource management and conservation. While building the accessibility channel between India and Lanka, several of Kutumb's interns, who Sugriva lovingly referred to as the 'Vanar Sena', had been working on network building and 'feet on the street' marketing. It was alongside the interns that some sideline projects were allotted to college projects in the name of the 'Squirrel Champions' wherein small-scale branding activities had to be proposed for small scale enterprises and a small gift prize was to be awarded for the winner.

" What will these little, inexperienced squirrel champions bring what we are not doing already?" A couple of interns had taunted the idea when first spoken about. However, as Jamba had prophesied, in the long term, a whole lot of buzz had generated from the on-campus activities and created a lot of traffic on the Expo network from small-scale entrepreneurs and freelancing consultants. "This is what resource management will bring to you, Lakshman," Ram had spoken with a humble appreciation of his little army. "While for them, it is a huge deal to be recognised on an international platform, for us, it is an opportunity to build unique and effective ideas at an affordable cost." With little steps of conservation, Ram and his team had managed to build a resource pool and save enough of their bootstrapped money to give the Grand Entrepreneurial Expo their best shot, delving into a space outside of their territory, where a man, with all his lustre and wealth awaited.

Ravan's wealth, as it was turning out, was a lot of facade and very little liquidity. The CRIF – a Centre for Research in International Finance – had already rejected his request for loan, owing to the bad credit score and unsatisfying audit results. Despite the amount of money spent on shutting mouths and approving contracts, Ravan had slowly built a reputation about himself that did not justify the kind of risks he expected his clients to take for him.

With several desperate attempts and failed requests, Ravan was beginning to realise that he was not going to have an easy time facing Ram and his troop at the Expo. The whole plan he had crafted about dazzling all the participants in the Expo with his glamorous exhibitions and an additional elite invitation to the leaders for a social dinner, was falling flat because of his under-estimation of the scenario he had found himself walking into. Had it been any other entrepreneur, he would probably have stopped in his tracks while he could and worked on the resurrection of what remained of Head Hunters. Ravan, however, was drunk with arrogance and driven with power. The position of admitting mistakes with humility and retracing his steps did not come naturally to him. Distraught with desperation, Ravan prepared to go against Ram in the Expo, putting his mind to wring the last of his muscle, with the attempt of putting together at least a position of respect in the public eye.

In the world of enterprise, financial sustenance is more a matter of choice than chance. A business owner, irrespective of his financial position, can take calls that are either too demanding or too frugal with respect to the account status. The key is to find and priorities your focus areas of investment. If the return is worthy of its investments, there is no doubt that opportunities should not be missed, even if it means going out on a limb. On the other hand, investments that seem glamorous or even trendy should not be made just because they seem like a safe bet or are seen to be the trendy choice. This only leads to brand confusion and diversion from the focus points. Lack of funds are actually a blessing in disguise because they encourage a sense of innovation, urgency and value of the available resources. Ownership and accountability built in your team will go a long way in earning loyalty and efficiency, thereby building a culture that is not just money conscious, but aware of the all the resources being utilised by the organisation.

10

When the Time is Ripe

Things had been looking up in Lanka for the entire team of Kutumb. With the buzz created by the Grand Entrepreneurial Expo, a lot of traffic and attention had been drawn to the available resources and possibilities. This was a booming time for all young talent across the globe to venture into the country.

"Ram, I have been sending out feelers with my friends in the government and heard that with the leading party opening up to join hands with multinational companies, there is a revolutionary policy review happening to allow foreign nationals to mushroom business models in the country, with the condition of allowing for proprietorship to be with domestic nationality. This works perfectly in our favour; we should launch the Kutumb partnership right away," Sugriva had suggested to the maestro. With the help of Lakshman's managerial skills and Vibhishan's insight into Lankan administration, this would not be too difficult to establish. However, the leadership's response was not as enthusiastic as Sugriva would have expected.

"Brother Sugriva, this is a very useful information you have brought to us. But we must not jump up to actions without making a well-thought conclusion on the consequences first," Ram explained kindly. "There is a whole herd of entrepreneurs dying to dive into the business spectrum at Lanka, what with the whole world's attention at the Expo. And mind you, it is not going to be very difficult for them to fulfil the criteria of establishing ground here either." Although Ram knew that they had the circumstances, their groundwork, experience and Vibhishan's unparalleled expertise and alliances in Lanka on their side, it would not be a unique achievement, even though unmatchable in quality.

"For any venture to hit the market at a sweet spot, it is imperative to have your timing right." Jamba began with drawing a ray on the whiteboard. "Too early and the market will not be conducive to receive the idea; too late and the market will have already seen the idea and you will just be a follower." Jamba had seen several business ideas spring into the market and be dismissed to the pavement despite being brilliant and efficient. Simply because they had not been able to time their step right.

"Right now is the time for us to work underground. The buzz is created, people are expecting something. But there has to be enough space and scope in the market to accept our co-working venture. That will come with the right people on our side." Ram seconded Jamba. He had a plan in mind, and had already chalked out the logistics. While the team Kutumb at the Lanka base camp worked out the operational details, continued with exploring and strengthening contacts, Ram would head to join the master investor Shiva and incubation specialist Durga in their global convention for rising entrepreneurs. The dynamic duo had set out on a tour and Ram intended to follow them and grab their attention towards Kutumb. He wanted them to notice his endeavours to win their support before he charged into an open battle against Ravan in his own home field.

Thus, leaving the reigns of homework in the trusted hands of his team, Ram left for nine days. Alone. To find and win the ultimate support he needed. This was not going to be easy. Durga was as meticulous in her selections as she was experienced in gauging through the end of a business idea. Ram would have to plan way ahead, since he would have to stay focussed, give up on everything else and prove his dedication and strength enough to attract not only the attention but enough interest of Durga to want to battle against the current interests of Lanka towards Ravan. The whole map of the encounter, eventual taking over of all the structured associations and alliances of Ravan would happen in due course. With the help of Hanuman's extensive homework, Ram had been able to chalk out the strengths and weaknesses of the leading businesses of different domains in Lanka. Knowing the strategic links and how to tap them would prove worthy.

"There is no doubt, Ram, that most of Ravan's partners and clients are not happy with his work. But they will never come out in the open against him unless it comes across that they were forced to do so. That can only happen if the country's leaders make it obvious that the entrepreneurial waves are changing. And for decisions to come from that high up, he would need a lot of influence to expose Ravan's wrong doings. That is where

Durga and Shiva came into the picture. It was in the government's best interest to allow foreign investors. It was in the interest of the foreign investors to march into the country. Their only roadblock was Ravan's scandals. Nobody wanted to get into that mess and have to scratch the corrupt leader the wrong way."

"The only way is to show them enough proof of Ravan's wrong doings and to convince them that there is someone better to replace his inefficiencies," Jamba and Ram had been discussing the plan of action. "We will move in strategically." The roll-out had begun a long while ago, with the massive PR of the Grand Expo that had attracted attention towards Lanka. Now, it was time to prove the gaps in Ravan's rule while establishing a roadmap to replacement, one that was in the interest of all.

Thus, the team split into two, began working on deconstruction as well as reconstruction of identities. While one worked in favour of Kutumb's brand value, the other worked against Ravan's malicious means under the blanket of the Head Hunters. The PR agency that had been working with Ram since the beginning of Kutumb, had partnered up with the small and old-school media houses of Lanka. "These are the roots that connect to the old generation, the ones that rely on conventional means of information," Sugriva had advised the in-house marketing team.

On the other hand, it was the digital marketing branch that had started working with the younger generation, in colleges, new startups, incubation centres, etc., who were more likely to join the trend, once it had caught enough reputation. "A lot of our response quality is dependent on Ram's reputation. At this stage, we must step up to make sure that the way the population perceives him is built on transparency and honesty, something they have been completely missing on the part of Ravan's reign."

The strategies were getting stronger with every step. In Ram's absence, communications were established through radio campaigns. PR activities were used in small, yet significant ways; they were subtle enough to stay reliable, but prominent enough to catch people's attention. Drives were run for capacity building of marginally educated population of the rural world. Free incubation centres were run in universities where students could not afford expensive guidance counsellors. While such activities were covered and advertised at subtle levels, always voiced through the beneficiaries instead of the organisers, there was another wave of activities going on behind the stage, where business propositions were being shared with stakeholders, gauging readiness and operational feasibility of setting up centres in Lanka. All timed in the right direction, with desired effect on reputation being earned through PR activities, and the buzz the Expo had rolled into motion, Lanka was slowly and steadily building up a momentum that would turn into a wave for Kutumb to ride on.

In the meanwhile, Ram had gotten himself on-board with a dedicated and exclusive convention to be in sync with Durga. His endeavours began with building alliances with all the c-founders who were running along with Durga, and were responsible for investigating and evaluating the businesses that aspired to work with the Nine Sister's alliance (what the powerful team was popularly known as).

One by one, for nine days, Ram met each and every member of the alliance, bringing to the table each segment of his business idea and existing model. "How do you plan on expanding?" Skandmata, Head of Sales venture, had enquired.

"By de-centralising our operational centres, down to the very basics, thereby cutting operational costs and increasing scale with local relevance," Ram responded with a studied confidence.

"How will the community benefit?" Siddhidatri, the Welfare Visionary enquired.

"By building capacity and employing a hundred percent of resources from the community. This will be a venture for the people and by the people. That is the very root of Kutumb," his reply was backed with the example of existing Kutumb model running in other locations.

There was little left to doubt or questioning. Just like everything else Ram did, his efforts were transparent and honest, thereby reflecting the earnestness of his intent and projections. For nine days, Ram travelled with Durga's entourage, answering questions, brainstorming and bringing up the SWOT analysis he had with regards to Lanka's current state of affairs.

"If you do not help Kutumb spread in Lanka, either Ravan will manipulate a way into using the new policies into his favour and continue with his greedy and corrupt exploitation of the country, or other, inefficient powers will try to overtake, battling each other into tatters. In either case, the masses are going to suffer, beaten up by the economy on one end and battered state of unemployment on the other." Ram spoke while presenting his deck on the final day, with Durga.

"Remember Ram, everyone speaks a language their heart listens. While most of our stakeholders believe in facts and numbers, Durga believes in intent and emotions, that is the connect you will want to look at. That is the angle she will most be appealed with." He remembered Jamba's words loud and clear as he made his speech. Durga sat listening to his arguments patiently. Having heard the news recently and knowing well enough the state Lanka had been pulled into because of Ravan's mismanagement, she viewed Ram's intervention as a divine design, meant for mutual benefit. It was not going to be a difficult decision to make, especially after Ram had brought along all proof of Ravan's malicious practices and corrupt means for having bagged several projects.

"The only speed breaker now, is getting the bureaucrats on our side. The population has already been gearing itself up for the changes that are about to come." Ram explained to Durga in the conclusion of his presentation. "This is not just a venture for you or a business opportunity for me, although that purpose is generously served, but also a respite that the Lankan population eagerly awaits and rightfully deserves. I am going to do everything in my capacity to restore the country its rightful golden state it once boasted of." There was sincerity and passion in Ram's eyes. His voice had hit home with Durga, who was intrigued, to say the least, by the possibilities of what lay ahead for the country, as well as for the numinous business opportunities that lay ahead once the doors for entrepreneurial world in Lanka opened up.

She stared straight at Ram and then, slowly gave him her famous go ahead nod. "You take care of the population. I will take care of the bureaucrats." She smiled, getting up from across the conference table. "You have my blessings and support for the execution. You will have the introductory meeting with the government branch in a couple of days." She assured and walked out.

All the endeavour had been brought to a sudden jolt with that one meeting with Durga. The homework seemed to have paid off. Meditation, patience and strategy had all built up to conjoin to this momentous timing when the government had aligned with the media and the population to open up a bouquet of opportunities for people. All Ram had to do now was to follow the timing, the track and soon, he would be brought face to face with their most awaited moment.

Timing is very critical at the time of any business introduction. You cannot go in too early, if the market is not ready and you definitely cannot go late, once the market has got a leading product to follow. Timing is not necessarily an involuntary flow that you jump into. Often, the right environment and conditions have to be created to kick start your business. This requires meticulous study of the market trends, keeping upbeat with the demands of the moving world, and above all, predicting the turns of the demands, based on a) the advancements of governing factors such as technology, governance, economy and b) the strengths and weaknesses of your competitors and complementary products. It is only wise to stay up-to-date with the ecosystem you are skirting and make an informed and primed plunge when you have prepped up with all your foundation steps.

11

Getting Ahead of the Game

"I am coming back next week. Our mission with Durga was successful. She has agreed to give us the backing we need with the government of Lanka," Ram called Lakshman with a practiced sense of peace in his voice. "This means we have an official go-ahead with operation Lanka," he explained to Lakshman, Jamba and Sugriva as everyone joined in on speakerphone on Lakshman's indication.

"This is great news, Ram. Everything we have been gearing up for will amount to our final steps towards Ravan." Jamba spoke half to Ram and half to the team of reliable people sitting in front of him. "This is where all our homework is going to come in handy." Jamba was already thinking ahead about the next steps. "Before we meet Ravan in the actual face-off with the rest of the stakeholders, we will have to prepare ourselves with all the things he can attack us with." It was going to be a strategic and categorial process, one that demanded meticulous attention, the details and one that would ask of Ram and his team to push their emotional, mental and physical capacity like never before.

The team went on into an extensive brainstorming session. "We will need to divide our work force into different domains. We can cover maximum ground if we all tap into each of our expertise," Lakshman began with the categorisation.

Ram was quite impressed with the initiatives his team had been taking in his absence. Shiva, during his last meeting with Ram, had clearly guided him to let other people take the front line of leadership. "I know it feels like it is much easier to guide and lead the way. But if you want a sustainable journey, not just for yourself but your organisation, what I would recommend for you is to build leaders, give people ownership and let them take risks, along with the accountability of the risks. This will help the journey be more meaningful, learned and long-term."

Ram knew instantly that he was on the right track. The man who he adored and admired for his leadership skills was telling him what he had felt in his heart to be the right thing to do. "You barely ever see me in action. I am mostly in the background. The idea is to give people the feeling that you do trust them and let them carry on. This is what builds second generation leaders in any organisation."

"So, since I am stuck here, we will be losing on critical time before our official encounter with Ravan. I don't know how to manage that from here." Ram played his card on the con-call with the team. This was his chance for the team to pick up on their own.

"There is nothing for you to worry about, Ram," Sugriva spoke confidently. "You have a solid team at work here. We are anyway halfway through our strategic action plan. You should not worry about us and carry on." As Sugriva assured Ram, he looked across at Jamba, Lakshman and Hanuman, who were all nodding vehemently in support, each confident and happy with the responsibilities being pushed their way. Assuring Ram that they would get back to him if they needed any guidance or solutions, his team hung up and turned to discuss their next steps.

" I think I am only speaking for what everyone feels here. Vibhishan should be taking the lead of Kutumb's execution in Lanka. He knows the population and they know and respect him back. He also has all the insight that he will need to exercise once facing the team of Head Hunters. It is much better to have a face people know and trust rather than an outsider." This was a well-thought strategy. Keeping Vibhishan the face of Kutumb in Lanka meant that they could dodge a lot of bullets that Ravan would shoot their way.

" To be a powerful brand, you need to have a story that connects with people and helps you win confidence in their hearts. Vibhishan has that story. He is the fighter, the loyalist and the man who cared much more for his country and organisation than his personal interests." Lakshman spoke showing off the virtual headlines that would lead all media as Vibhishan would become the face of Lanka's revolution.

Sugriva had immense skills to mobilise the community. Just as he would stand up and walk amidst his team, people, especially youngsters, would follow him and seek guidance. This was not just true for people in Kutumb, but for wherever Sugriva had been going to associate with the crowd in Lanka. He would head marketing and get all links ready for the team to launch. "You will need to find out everything that Ravan has been doing with the leading marketing agencies of Lanka and top that with originality. We have to get the media platforms on our side. We need to know everything before it hits the public forums." Jamba spoke to Sugriva, who headed out immediately.

Hanuman was an expert in problem solving, hands down; the best person available for firefighting or even putting out the sparks before they turned into flame. "I will look for all possible attacks that Ravan can have on us and have the team prepare for defences for that. If we know what is coming our way, we can render his accusations ineffective by our shear preparedness and confidence." Hanuman was already talking like the solutions, man he was known to be.

Lakshman was already on his toes for collaboration with people who had earlier teamed up with the Head Hunters. With an informal go ahead from Durga and Ram, he launched into setting up contracts, looking up locations for centres and finishing the code that would be needed to install Kutumb centres in Lanka.

"Ram, I just wanted to update you about some new information that has come to us so that you are aware and prepared about what to expect here." Jamba called Ram after getting a detailed report from Sugriva about the latest developments in Head Hunters. "There is going to be a deliberate and organised attempt of defamation from 'unknown sources' towards Kutumb. They will start with random reports of malpractices and bad experiences with Kutumb and eventually lead to a trend on social media. They are doing this in an attempt to discredit your association with the government and other corporate partners. We have been told that there are going to be attempts of slander against you with respect to what happened between Bali and you. That is not all, even Sita is going to be brought to alter on social media as having being abandoned by you."

Ram listened with patience, both analysing the depth of the threat as well as admiring the intelligence and diligence of his team. "I understand. What do you think we should be doing?" Ram was determined to let his team take the lead in this crusade against Lanka.

" We already have planned the action we are going to take, Ram. We will slowly and categorically start releasing stories of Ram and Kutumb and what goes on here at a personal and emotional level. We will cover the lives of the people we have touched so far and what the common people think about us. This will help us build a persona for Kutumb that cannot be breached by frivolous gossip." Hanuman explained with drafts of interventions. "I would also recommend that whenever any attack is made on either the professional or personal space of anyone in Kutumb, we should not pay too much attention to the media propaganda, so as not to give it more attention than it deserves." Hanuman further proposed his recommendation of sending out feelers for all members of Kutumb, to revisit their conduct, both online and offline with their environment, to make sure that there was nothing objectionable that could be drawn to maligning them. "Meanwhile, we have started working on PR strategies to bring to light the welfare work we have been doing for all these years. This is not the time to stay humble about our ideologies but to propagate them for people to connect with us."

The internal planning of Kutumb was just as rigorous as the fine tuning of the image of Kutumb on all public forums. Lakshman proposed the next steps in terms of operations that the bigger challenges of the coming times would demand of them. "I am talking about building the capacities of this team, knowing they are about to be exposed to one of the biggest and most challenging exposures the team would have experienced so far. Prepping them for 'war'," Laksham spoke about his plan of sending selected members of all teams for exposure visits, online courses and conferences, not only to lobby up with people, but also to fine tune their skills that would prep them with simulated situations of what waits for them, as well as how such situations are dealt with by experts."

Ram nodded, happy with having all their grounds covered and just as satisfied to see his team gear up with such lustre to climb over the next level of challenge. After the long and exhausting schedule with Durga, he finally took her blessings and headed towards Lanka, to meet his team and to brace himself for the face-off with Ravan.

If you want to race against your competitors, you have to plan five steps ahead of where your opponent might be positioning themselves or planning their future. This requires meticulous research, covering all grounds and preparing for the upcoming challenge even before your team has been presented with the challenge. A good strategy is not to run with a capacity of your current position, but with one that will get you ready for the next five years. Knowing your competitors and preparing yourself based on not just your strengths but also their weaknesses is the best strategy, when you are pitching to be the market leader. Reading up on what is happening in the market gives you an idea of what plans and developments are happening and why. This gives an insight into why certain decisions were made. Once the pattern is understood, it can be possible to track the mindset and strategising techniques of your market leaders, thereby giving you the opportunity to think ahead of them.

12

Encountering the Competition, Head-on

The day had finally arrived when all the hard work, the strategic alliances, research and development would fall into action. Ram had arrived in Lanka a couple of days ago after seeking guidance from Durga.

"Rest assured Ram, you will have my support at the board meeting and you will also find yourself some allies in the government who have agreed to overthrow Ravan's inefficient and corrupt tyrannical autonomy in Lanka's business." Durga had spoken off the record. True to her words, Durga had come up with pre-prepared alliances, all ready and willing to side with Ram when the need so arose.

As everyone geared up for the day's unfolding, the onsite team of Kutumb, led by Lakshman, got ready. This would be the network that would provide live sharing of the market to the board, scan approval ratings, and bring real time reactions. In all, it would let the board understand the responses of the market with oncoming deals, involving perspectives of all stakeholders. Representatives from the Ministry of Education were present in the conference room, as punctual as always. Ram was there with Jamba too. His secretaries were reviewing all presentations and data points. People from Head Hunters had started pouring in, fashionably late and flouting all norms of decorum. Amidst a scene of chaos, a parade of officials and a bouquet of documentation, there was a sudden storm of silence. The doors opened and in walked a tall, strong and sharp looking man, with his entourage of assistants and consultants, all humming with a resonance of power. "When you do meet him, it will be like nothing you have ever experienced before," Hanuman had explained to the team of juniors in Kutumb. "You cannot overcome how much you would want to hate him, at the same time, you cannot help being in awe with his persona, his strength and his sheer presence."

Jamba nodded at Ram, with a knowing understanding. It was a classic move in the world of business. The whole concept of branding circulated around this charisma. "Branding is not just about what your product or service looks like to the outside world. It reflects in every action you take, every handshake you make and every rule you make in and outside your office space." Jamba had explained the whole power-dynamics to Ram and Lakshman as they began preparing for the final encounter. The whole scenario unfolded itself just the way it has been predicted. Ravan, true to his image, enamoured everyone with his smile, his larger than life image and his deliberately slow and piercing gaze. His power was already working at a psychological level. It was critical for the whole drama around Ravan, after all, to be perceived as intimidating, as someone who could not be refused and especially as someone who held the entitlement of being right, always.

There were several people in that conference room who knew, in great detail, the follies of this drama. They knew all of Ravan's maliciousness, his corruption and his actions that had harmed thousands of honest simpletons. And yet, most of them could not help being impressed by his charisma. Ram knew then why it had failed his reasoning to understand Ravan's indescribable success. Despite all of his flaws, Ravan had created an irrefutable persona. That is why he insisted on meeting all of his clients in person to crack a deal and never engaged with people through online modes. He was a man well aware of his strengths.

And strengths was what he began his pitch with. "Ladies and gentlemen, Head Hunters has never needed an introduction. Everyone knows our outreach, our performance and the sheer number of accounts we handle on a day-to-day basis. I am hoping the newfound policies will keep in mind everything I have done with and for the governing members sitting here," Ravan spoke just as much with his eyes, staring down at people who were in one way or another, indebted to Ravan through big or small favours. Deploying his classic game plan, Ravan began with his presentations, with his entourage following methodical instructions in a well-rehearsed synchronicity. Ravan was set to charm his way through the meeting, influencing and bending decisions, as always, to ensure that Head Hunters walk away with the highest chunk of benefits from the new education and incubation policies. However, it was this very Hubris that would lead him into a trap he was setting for himself. As Ravan went on enumerating his financial success, the number of partners he was working with and his achievements, all decorated with awards.

While most of the panel found themselves being influenced by his accolades, Ram, who had foreseen this, had come prepared with his own share of homework to pitch against Ravan's claims. “So you say that the financial growth in the last two years has been over 12%. That is monumental, Ravan. But if I understand correctly, a lot of this growth has been built on credit. And from what Head Hunter's current credit score mentions, you have been down by 22%!” Ram claimed, with a level head and a calm tone. This had never happened before. Ravan had never been questioned or apprehended, let alone accused of lying in a meeting before. Heads turned as the power dynamics suddenly shifted in the room. This was when Durga's friends from the Reserve Bank brought out their slides on the screen and showed everyone the downfall Head Hunters had had in the last five years. Grabbing the moment, Ram tossed in more examples of Ravan's deficit, one after another, all with proofs. Ravan stood at the head of the table, in the middle of his very decorated presentation, confused about what was going on. Just last week, he had sat his department heads down, assessing the situations from each front before he faced the music. In his proposition of ideas, he had asked how feasible things sounded for the staff on-ground. However, Ravan's impression of taking feedback had never been the best. His arrogance and ego had been infamous amidst his staff. And while he had taken pride in how much he could intimidate and command fear in his organisation, drowned in his Hubris, Ravan never realised he had chronically distanced himself from the realities in his organisation and about the practicalities of his progress.

"Are you sure, Ravan, that the partners you boast of are really on your side?" Ram batted carefully. Presenting the latest data then, he played his cards, revealing how many of Ravan's claimed partners had joined hands with Kutumb. It was then that Ram began unfolding all the cards he had in his deck, bringing down, one after another, the Head of Operation, Head of Finance, Head of Marketing… all proposals pitched by Ravan kept falling flat. With Durga's background work on alliance and Ram's diligent research, every claim Ravan made was met with a counter argument, along with solid proofs.

"I do not know where you are getting your information from, Ram, but I would like to see all these real time reporting you keep talking about!" Ravan spoke slyly. He knew Ram was up to something but he was, after all, a mastermind himself and did not hesitate in bringing out foul means where needed.

"I thought you'd never ask," Ram said, unknowingly falling into Ravan's malicious trap. "Ladies and gentlemen, we have our sources live at the stock market and in the education board, where live data are fed into the system. This is where all of Ravan's fraud statements will be proved false." Ram had no idea, however, that the moment he would log in to the server, something unexpected would happen. Lakshman's face appeared on the video pop up, greeting everyone in the room, but before he could even start presenting the data, something went wrong, blacking out the entire network, stranding Lakshman on the verge of disconnection, making him lose all sharing capacity. Although it looked like an accident, this was a well-marked strategy by Ravan, keeping his hacking team ready to bridge into Ram's server the moment he came online.

"What happened, Ram? Is this some kind of a strategy to waste our time? I would be scared to think that the government is inclined towards such inefficiencies to build Lanka's economic growth!" Ravan mocked Ram and the entire panel.

A wave of panic struck team Kutumb, with people trying desperately backend, to patch through the network. They were losing precious market time, which closed in an hour. If they were not able to reconnect, Ravan would be able to go back at the end of the day and forge all data again, like he had been doing with the rest of his claims. And yet, in this moment of chaos, Ram sat patient and calm, working his way backwards to finding a solution.

"Jamba, it seems like there is some corrupt link in the server. What can be done to fix it?" Ram asked his tech-expert.

Jamba, who had already been calculating the details in his head called Hanuman immediately. "Hanuman, get to Drona, the server hub, find the re-patch router, the one that resembles the codes of the affected one, and take them to Lakshman to relocate the server. This will redirect any virus that may have hacked into our system and bring us back online."

Now, Hanuman was no expert, but he knew how to follow orders and manage resources. Dumping his struggles, he rushed over to Drona, their tech-hub and began searching meticulously for the re-patch router. "I have no idea what it looks like! How am I going to make sure I find the right set?" Hanuman contemplated for a flash and immediately decided to do what he did best, crisis management. "Jamba, I could not find the router but I am bringing the entire Drona to Lakshman. We will be able to select the router with the correct frequencies there and relocate," Hanuman contacted his mentor while already on the go.

Lakshman, who was struggling with a network that was fast being attacked by viruses, was on the edge of losing all his data. "I am here, Lakshman!" Hanuman exclaimed, laying down the entire hub of wires and routers before him. The team jumped to it immediately, finding the right frequency, as Hanuman had predicted, and finding the re-patch device. Within no time, Lakshman recovered his server.

While Ravan was gloating in the conference room, throwing his weight with all the fake data his team had built up for him, Lakshman's interface popped back up on the screen, and he immediately started sharing data from the central system, with about five minutes remaining! "As you can see, ladies and gentlemen, the drift of the population has been towards in-house resourcing instead of out-sourcing to other countries in the last six month, contrary to what Ravan has been pitching," Ram rushed to action immediately. "Thus making it extremely critical and viable to focus our budget and policy towards domestic capacity building," Ram concluded.

This got very appreciative nods from the panel that had already been making up its mind towards allowing for a free and promoted implementation of capacity building, allowing inflow of businesses from outside of Lanka instead of simply allowing for talents to drain from the country.

"But Kutumb is an outsider's club. Letting them in would be exploitative and untrustworthy," Ravan got defensive and desperate. He had been losing categorically and demeaningly, receiving blows to his ego, one after another.

This brought a kind smile on Ram's face, as though he was expecting this. "Yes, I have complete realisation that I am and will continue to be an outsider. For the rightful and efficient growth of the country, we need somebody who belongs here, someone who is a leader and is loved and trusted by all. I therefore present to you, Vibhishan." Ravan's younger brother walked into the conference room with a gentle smile on his face, as though he had just arrived home. Ravan looked at him, stunned. He had not been prepared for this move and suddenly realised that the whole world he had built around him was crashing down and he could do nothing about it.

It is very important to have your vision and mission clear in your head. To do that, it is critical to stay connected to the reality of your business. You may think you are on the path to success and yes, you may actually be on the path of success, but there is a very thin line between arrogance and confidence. It helps to stay close to people who criticise you and push you towards evaluating yourself from time to time. If you keep yourself deprived from such evaluation, it will be difficult to assess the success of your enterprise and give you the opportunity to grow further. In dealing with strong competition, the best strategy is the simplest one. Like a student, you should study your market, your competition and understand their strengths, weaknesses and strategies. Instead of attacking them, if you prepare yourself in accordance, not only will you be following the ethical practice of business, but you will actually be able to tackle your market better. Your ethos and principles reflect in many forms, from your services to your conduct and that is what is most obviously perceived by your consumers and alliances.

13

Emerging as the Alpha

Watching Vibhishan walk in was definitely the last nail in Ravan's coffin. No one had ever witnessed colour drain from a man's face as fast before. He had driven his own brother away a while ago. Even if he would not admit it to himself, in his sheer arrogance, Ravan had forgotten all about his brother, about the insult he had thrown at Vibhishan's face or the persistent goodwill with which Vibhishan had tried to counsel him towards the rightful path in enterprise. "Your problem, stupid brother, is that you are too spineless to think beyond the rules and too weak to challenge power. You do not understand when to keep your mouth shut or when to stop boasting your know-it-all attitude." Ravan had thrashed Vibhishan in front of an entire room full of employees during one of the review meetings.

"But Ravan, I am just trying to show you that this will not go a long way in favour of Head Hunters," Vibhishan had pleaded, still unaware of his brother's intentions. Ravan had been looking for excuses to pick up fights with his younger sibling, who, he saw as nothing more than a road block. And this particular session had given him more than enough ammunition to take it all out on Vibhishan. "I think I have had enough of you. I no longer have doubts in declaring that you are nothing but a burden and a nuisance in my path to success. It is best that you leave

Head Hunters right away. Forget Head Hunters, I think it is best if you leave Lanka for good and never show me your face again!"

Even today, watching his brother take strong, calculated steps into the conference room reminded him of the sorry figure of his abandoned brother, who had taken one last look at Ravan before he left the premises. That look had no anger, no sense of vengeance. Ravan had not understood what that look meant. But today, looking into those eyes again, he saw that look once more. Today, he understood that it was a look of pity that Vibhishan felt for his arrogant brother, who he knew was unaware of the grave he had dug for himself.

"Hello friends, it is so good to be home!" Vibhishan exclaimed with utmost sincerity when he entered to meet all the known faces. Despite the obvious discomfort on the Head Hunters' side, Vibhishan was embraced with smiling faces and warm hugs by those who knew his heart and how much he had really worked for the benefit of the organisation, as well as Lanka.

"Ladies and gentlemen, as I was saying, I truly understand and appreciate your concern for the need of an insider who will take forth the implementation of policies here in Lanka," Ram addressed the gathering after giving them due time to take in Vibhishan's appearance and to settle back down into their seats. "And that is why, I can think of no better person that Vibhishan, who has decided to come back to Lanka and volunteer himself for this extremely critical and responsible position."

Heads were already nodding in approval. Nobody had imagined that Ram's master stroke would come in the form of Ravan's own brother, his once closest ally and someone who knew and understood the nuances of the organisation, perhaps even more than Ravan (what with his blindsided arrogance). Ram had deliberately kept his secret weapon hidden till the end, because he knew that he would really have to time his strategy in a way that it is not too early for Ravan to come up with a plan of defence and not too late for the panel to have already come up with a solution of their own, in which case, it might become difficult to sway their decision. And thus, just when Ravan's side had been weakened and a need for a new front-runner had emerged, Ram had conveniently positioned Vibhishan into a spot from where he could appear to be not just the only available choice, but the best available choice for them.

"Wait a minute, you are not suggesting that I am done with, are you?" Ravan roared in agitation. "You may all be under the misconception that Head Hunters has flaws in its records, but you cannot circle them back to me. On the contrary, I have a spectacular and fault-free record, both with the government, as well as the public." Ravan was up to his sly and fraudulent tricks again. "You can check all the documents and history you have on me!" He was still going by the media image he had created for himself, which enabled him to get away with a lot of things in the past. Just then, Jamba switched open his system and began reconnecting his display screen to that of the conference room. Vibhishan, who had been keeping quiet this whole time, got up to connect to the server on the screen Jamba had opened before him. Everybody turned to face the live screen as Vibhishan started typing in Ravan's credentials for what looked like a digital locker.

"There are things kept hidden in the stomach of your being, Ravan. Unfortunately for you, I am someone who was once very close to you. I therefore know all the truth behind the facade you have created for yourself," Vibhishan spoke calmly as he typed away, opening pages after pages on screen. Ravan's eyes widened in dismay and disbelief to what he had completely forgotten in his overconfidence. The pages on the screen revealed every big and small accounts, every transaction, every detail of the tenders and bills Ravan had manipulated or bribed for or had undercover, all on his personal ownership.

"Not only does this prove Ravan to be responsible for all the fraudulent practices that have been going on at Head Hunters that we discussed, but also connects him to several other corrupt stunts, even outside of the organisation and outside of Lanka as well!" Ram declared categorically, enunciating his words with every proof drawn from Ravan's personal belly account that Vibhishan had retracted.

With this final blow, everyone turned to Ravan to see if the arrogant leader still had any defence left to annoy them or to embarrass himself. It was quite unsettling to see his head hung in shame, his hands clutching his stomach with dear life as he heaved a huge sigh of submission. "I have nothing more to say. I know that I am beaten and I will now step down from my position as the CEO of Head Hunters, resign from all my position on the boards and hand myself over to law-enforcement for any actions that I am liable for."

Ravan and Ram exchanged a long, deep look, from one leader to another, from one who had declared and the other who had submitted, from one who had won and the one who had conceited. In that one, short moment, Ram knew and understood all of Ravan's intelligence, his ambition and his unending drive towards power and desperation to be on top. Ravan, on the other hand, realised all of Ram's honesty, his purity of intent and his commitment to doing what was right. In that one moment, both Ram and Ravan held respect for each other.

"There is not much debate to decide where we head from here. Ravan will be handed over to the Ministry of Finance for clearing all debts and charges that will now be filed against him, based on all the evidence collected against him by you and by those shared by Durga." More such cases were coming to light and several people had begun speaking up, the representatives of the board were in unison on their decision. "Vibhishan, we hope you will take over Head Hunters, as Ram promised, and replace Ravan on all panels, to help us draft new policies to change foreign investment and enterprise engagement in Lanka."

Watching all of this finally roll over smoothly, Ram stepped out of the conference room, out of the building and back to Kutumb's base camp, where Sita has been waiting to join him after watching the whole chain of events play out. Hugging Ram intently, Sita wiped her tears, "I am so glad you are here, Ram. I am so glad that Lanka and Ravan got the justice they deserved. And above all, I am so glad that I am back to where I belong!" Ram wiped her cheeks with kind hands and encouraged her to help team Kutumb wrap up, now that their work in Lanka was done.

"Lakshman, I think it is time we head back to Ayodhya, now that we have established everything the way we wanted. With the allies we have built and business we have grown, I think I am ready to embrace the past and get back to working with the simple and deprived people who taught me to work in the rightful manner in the first place. But before we go, I want you to go and meet Ravan, and ask him all about the policies and strategies he had in mind for Lanka." Lakshman was shocked to hear Ram asking to seek Ravan's counsel. "I know what you think brother, but Ravan is one of the most intelligent entrepreneurs I have ever encountered, albeit a misguided one. There is a lot to learn from him, and believe me, he will be willing to impart his knowledge just as openly to you as you will be willing to receive it.

Knowing your competition can reveal deep-seated advantages that can come in handy at the right time. It is helpful to have some strategies up your sleeve that you do not go around revealing on public forums without pre-meditative timing. It is critical to understand what information you reveal and when you reveal it, to reap the best possible fruits from its impact. Another very important thing as an entrepreneur is to leave aside your baggage of ego and to recognise true value when you see it. It is only the most honest and most humble leaders who can see the truth behind their friends and foes and draw learnings from all their experiences, no matter what their position is.

14

The Return to Ground Zero

"I can't believe we are finally doing this!" Lakshman exclaimed as the trio landed at the airport. It had been a long and tiring journey, all the way from Lanka and yet, there had nothing been as refreshing and relaxing they had experienced in the last fourteen years of their exciting journey.

"What are some of the best moments you had in this tenure? I am curious to know," Ram asked his wife and his brother as they waited to de-board their plane. While Sita took her time to respond, Lakshman replied instantly. "I loved that there were learnings in everything we did. I loved that we started from scratch and built ourselves an empire that grew beyond geography and became a phenomenon that managed to change the policies and governance of a nation altogether…" Lakshman went on to enlist the gist of almost the whole of their experiences of fourteen years. It had been, after all, a memorable experience; one that had changed several lives and brought together a collection of people who were the best of their respective fields.

"Not only did we bring together excellence, but we also pushed each other towards achieving beyond excellence in all forms." Lakshman was all smiles.

Sita nodded patiently. She had been away for a considerable chunk of the experience that Kutumb experienced in the last year. However, she had been involved in the foundation days and had helped Ram and Lakshman build up the brand of Kutumb, helped coin the vision and mission of the organisation and helped put together the team that had now become the front runners of Kutumb across the world.

Sita was one to appreciate the deeper, more fundamental essence of life and respected the same qualities in Ram as well. "I admire you for standing up for your principles and what you knew to be right. I love that you took some very difficult decisions and stuck to the choices you made, despite how difficult things became on the way. More than anything else, I enjoyed being on the right side of the battle, watching people build and crumble around me, and I enjoyed knowing that nothing could shake us because we were on the right side." Sita looked at her husband and partner, admiring his unshaken spirit.

Ram smiled and nodded at his two true, honest and loyal friends who had stuck by his side with unconditional support and given up every comfort and luxury to be with him when the world around him had given up on him. He thought back about his days in Ayodhya, fourteen years ago, when he had been forced to leave because of the enforcements that had been exercised on him. He recalled the many people who had given him so much love and blessings even when he left his home town. Ram was drowned with unending memories of all the new friends and associations he had met in the last fourteen years, all unexpected or unintended. He thought of Sugriva, who had put so much faith in Ram, despite his desperate position and brought around his entire team of support staff because of his belief in Ram. He thought of the many victories he had earned on the way, big or small, whether it was winning their first tender or acquiring the entirety of a giant organisation like Head Hunters. Ram could see the entire montage of moments when he had to make tough decision, give up his personal comfort for the welfare of those around him; when he had to keep his morale high and put on a brave face even at the most challenging issues or in the worst of crisis.

"I am glad I had you two by my side, instilling confidence and strength in me. What means the most to me is that you always took the trouble of standing up for what you felt to be right and openly pointed out the points where you disagreed with me or felt that we were digressing from our intended path. For that, I will forever be grateful, that you were my strength when I myself was on the verge of finding myself weak and exhausted."

"I still do not understand why you came back, Ram. We had everything going on superbly for us there. We had established stellar relations in the market space and had no upcoming hurdles in our near future," Lakshman asked his brother as they began collecting their minimal luggage.

Despite their long stay away, the trio had barely engaged in luxury of possession. "Focus on what is underneath than what covers over the surface," their father had always told them. The principles had run home with the siblings. Luxury, in their head, had been knowledge, experiences and associations, not material possessions, labels and numbers.

"You know, brother, when I left from Ayodhya, I was positive. Not just because I knew we would make something of wherever we go, but I knew that it would be alright to come back at some point, if I just waited for the right time." Ram spoke, staring at something beyond the horizon. "When we had accomplished what we did, I knew we could come back, decentralise and work on different projects." Ram radiated confidence like never before.

After delegating work in Lanka, he had promoted Sugriva, Jamba and Vibhishan to go on and set their own divisions in different locations. "I have done everything I could possibly think of with you. I think you are all ready to make your own ground and set your own foundation with all the knowledge and experience we have shared with each other," Ram had parted with his friends after words of ultimate confidence.

He knew and understood that after achieving a certain level of success, it does not make any sense to hang on to the trumpet of success. "Instead," he explained to Lakshman as they stepped out of the airport and into the taxi line, "you have to know when you have saturated your vertical and when it is time to start expanding your business, both vertically and horizontally." And that is why, Ram, after all these years, had decided to take up the invitation of the Governor of Ayodhya to come back to Ayodhya for talks ever since Ram and Kutumb had made headlines in all leading newspapers, about his critical role in negotiations with the government of Lanka.

His best resources, most conducive ecosystem and all possible future alliances across verticals would all be found in Ayodhya. "Why stay put in the pretext of comfort when you know that stepping out will bring you a lot more lucrative results?" Ram would always challenge the complacence and limits of everyone around him and himself.

As the trio turned into the familiarity of their home street, the warm feeling of being home at long last really started sinking in. What they did not expect to see, was that the whole street was lit up with some kind of festivities all across the houses and stores. "It is not some kind of festival, is it?" Lakshman asked them. Every single house was lit up with lamps and decorations. As they stopped outside their old house, they saw an up and running board of 'Ram Enterprise' stationed proudly atop their old office. They could see a huge crowd of people standing in a gathering, bustling with excitement.

" Oh goodness, you guys are here!" Bharat ran to them even before they had entered the premise. He took his brothers into a tight embrace, tears streaming down his face. The rest of the crowd, friends and family of Ram, Sita and Lakshman followed, all overwhelming the trio with a million greetings, questions and compliments. This was indeed going to be a bright, well-lit and long night for everyone.

Amidst the tremendous chaos, laughter and conversations, Ram found himself heading back to Lakshman and Sita, who were catching up with Bharat. “I have been following all your work closely, Ram, and trying to reproduce as much of it here as possible under Ram Enterprises. Everything I have done, I have continued with the intention of preserving your principles and honour in this workplace, waiting for you to come back and start over,” Bharat looked expectantly at Ram, half-expecting him to scuff at the brother because of whom he had to leave all those years ago.

And yet, Ram smiled, patting his young brother's back, “I am so excited to learn everything from you that happened while we were gone!” he declared passionately. “So team, what should we do next, now that we are back to ground zero?” Ram asked looking at his most favourite people in the world as they all broke into a hearty laughter and began sharing their own plans for the next steps. With everything that had happened, while one journey had come to an end, it appeared that another had just begun for Ram and his entrepreneurial spirit.

The sign of a true and farsighted businessman is to continue with retrospection and introspection along with his trusted group of colleagues, friends or like-minded individuals. While it takes strength to make difficult choices, it takes even greater strength and wisdom to revisit them, analyse your strengths and weaknesses and derive your learnings. A critical part of the learning is to know when you have reached the epoch of your enterprise and grown in it as much as it is possible. This is the time to then start coming up with modifications, evolutions or diversifications to make the best of your enterprise and the opportunities that are arising from it. It is also equally important to have your employees grow just as much as your organisation does, and that is a sign of a healthy and loyal organisation culture that works for integral development.

By the same author

Non-Fiction

Fiction